D0164732

THE IMPRINT OF MAN

edited by
Emmanuel Anati

Also in this series:

Antonio Beltran
Rock art of the Spanish Levant

THE IMPRINT OF MAN

The Dawn of European Art

Published by the Press Syndicate of the University of Cambridge
The Pitt Building, Trumpington Street, Cambridge CB2 1RP
32 East 57th Street, New York, NY 10022, USA
296 Beaconsfield Parade, Middle Park, Melbourne 3206, Australia

Originally published in Italian as *I Piu' antichi artisti d'Europa* by Editoriale Jaca Book, Milan, 1981 and © Editoriale Jaca Book 1980

First published in English by Cambridge University Press (1982) as *The Dawn of European Art*
English translation © Cambridge University Press 1982

Printed in Italy

Library of Congress catalogue card number 81-21715

British Library Cataloguing in Publication Data
Leroi-Gourhan, André
The dawn of European art: an introduction to
palaeolithic cave painting.—(The imprint of man)
1. Cave-drawings—France 2. Palaeolithic period—France
1. Title II. I pin' antichi artisti d'Europe.
English III. Series
759.01'13'0944   N5310.5.F7

ISBN 0 521 24459 5

The Dawn of European Art

An Introduction to Palaeolithic Cave Painting

ANDRÉ LEROI-GOURHAN

Translated by Sara Champion

CAMBRIDGE UNIVERSITY PRESS

CAMBRIDGE
LONDON   NEW YORK   NEW ROCHELLE
MELBOURNE   SYDNEY

Contents

851455

LIBRARY
ALMA COLLEGE
ALMA, MICHIGAN

Introduction

Palaeolithic art was discovered at the beginning of the second third of the 19th century, simultaneously at Geneva (François Mayor's excavations at Veyrier) and in France (Brouillet's excavations at Le Chaffaud, Vienne). The works discovered consisted of two harpoons decorated with geometric figures at Veyrier and a reindeer metapodial engraved with two hinds at Le Chaffaud. Subsequently numerous decorated objects were dug up in caves, associated with worked flints and the bones of animals which in some cases had disappeared from our regions long before historical time. This clearly demonstrated the very early character of 'mobiliary' art, a term which is applied to all those decorated objects found in the layers successively formed in inhabited caves, rock shelters and open-air settlements. If mobiliary art was recognised relatively early (between 1860 and 1870), art on cave walls was not certainly identified until much later. In fact, the painted ceiling in the Altamira cave, discovered in 1879, was not accepted as authentic until the beginning of the 20th century. The main thrust of studies on prehistoric cave art for the last three-quarters of a century has been directed towards the establishment of a chronology and to a quest for the 'why?' of the works. There was a clear intention to concentrate on two aspects, the establishment of the limits in time, and the clarification of the meaning, of documents which stand at the beginning of a type of expression that has continued through writing to the present day. If plenty still remains to be discovered about the 'why?' of the symbols depicted on cave walls, almost everything remains to be said about the 'how?'.

Parietal palaeolithic art before 8000 BC would probably not just have been cave art but the simple fact is that evidence for its use in the open air has disappeared irretrievably. It is indeed impossible that palaeolithic man, who lived mainly in open air settlements, did not produce works of art on bark, skin, wood and stone blocks. The great mammoth bones (shoulder-blade and skull) from the Ukraine, decorated with geometric figures, are present as evidence to the contrary.

Prehistoric art is not simply restricted to the Palaeolithic (from about 35,000 to 8000 BC), for the prehistory of Europe lasted until the Iron Age in a current of technical and social evolution which proceeded progressively from the extractive economy of hunter–fisher–gatherers to the productive economy of agriculturalist–stockraisers. The boundary between these two fundamental forms of cultural life is imprecise in both time and space, but with the last manifestations of the last phase of the Würm glaciation, in the final Magdalenian, the last representatives of the palaeolithic world disappeared (as had already some time previously from our area the lion, the cave bear, the mammoth and the woolly rhinoceros). Parietal art ceased to develop further, the depths of caves were no longer visited, and drawings that one can link with certainty to the post-glacial are rare. In contrast, designs are found engraved on open air surfaces or exterior stone blocks from the Neolithic to the Iron Age and, in certain areas, up to the mediaeval period. This post-glacial art, called 'rupestral' because of the nature of its support, is quite different in style and subject matter from palaeolithic parietal art. The present work will not deal with rupestral art, except incidentally, but rather with the remarkable flourishing of palaeolithic works of art. Moreover, the subject will be limited to parietal art, as mobiliary art constitutes an area sufficiently distinct to be treated separately. Nevertheless this is the place to distinguish between decorated objects and plaques (of stone, ivory, bone and reindeer antler) which only serve as a support for decoration. It is as legitimate an approach as, for example, making separate studies, in Greek art, of great sculpture on the one hand and of pottery as a vehicle for decoration on the other. The two arts (parietal and mobiliary) share the important element of iconography, and the necessary comparisons will be made when they arise.

Whether prehistorians accept or deny the magic or religious character of the designs, or their deliberate or fortuitous placing in different parts of subterranean systems, all authors find themselves very generally agreeing that the images in the caves were the framework for an ideology which is expressed in symbols associated with fertility and the hunt. Though this minimal certainty has been achieved, studies diverge to reach the diametrically opposed theories either that the works, successively accumulated by chance over time, were the result of the practice of sympathetic magic, or that the pictures constitute a symbolic apparatus linked to the shape of the cave, a 'decoration' in which the different elements fill predetermined positions. In both theories it is clear that the thought processes which the figures represent are much more complex than was originally believed, so it seemed interesting to try out a less contentious area, that of the circumstances of actual production of the works. The large assemblages of figures like those at Lascaux, Les Trois-Frères, Altamira, Niaux, Ekaîn, Pech-Merle and Rouffignac, curious as it might seem, have never been subjected to any rigorous pictorial analysis, and one continues to talk of the Altamira ceiling as an artistic marvel without considering the balance between the figures as anything other than chance. Forgetting, perhaps temporarily, the entrancing yet impassioned area of 'why cave art?', an attempt is made in this book to identify, as a first stage, the questions still to be asked about the more material aspects of its execution (engraving, painting, sculpture) and on the role of the support. The analysis of form, and of the perception of time and space constitute the following stages and, in the absence of the textual meaning of the message, the construction of a model is attempted.

Technique

As an initial generalisation one can say that parietal works comprise engraving, sculpture and painting, though the three techniques are frequently combined. One can see laying-out lines engraved and covered over by painted figures, notably on the Altamira ceiling; painted sculptures such as at Angles-sur-l'Anglin; and paintings with engravings over as at Lascaux. Excision techniques (engraving and sculpture) in palaeolithic art show a quite remarkable technical coherence. Before the Solutrean, only a few parietal works can be dated with certainty. On the other hand, there are a number of blocks decorated by using a combination of deep engraving and pecking to achieve thick contours (Style I). Between these engraved blocks from the Aurignacian (c. 30,000–25,000 BC) and the already mature art of the Solutrean, the intermediate stages are still not well known. The dominant technique seems to have been fairly deep engraving (Pair-non-Pair) or fine engraving (Gargas). Painting from this period of Style II is almost unknown, but we are certain of its existence because of the presence of colouring materials as well as a few fragmentary painted figures.

ENGRAVING AND SCULPTURE

The expression of volume greatly preoccupied palaeolithic artists. Numerous examples show the use of natural relief in caves: a concave wall suggesting a bulging flank, the ridge in a wall used as a dorsal line or the drippings of stalactites integrated as animal feet demonstrate an interest in
29 volume which proves the existence of true bas-reliefs in the Solutrean and Magdalenian. Le Roc-du-Sers and Mouthiers in Charente, Le Cap Blanc in the Dordogne and the extraordinary assemblage at Angles-sur-l'Anglin were sculpted with hollows as much as ten centimetres deep
30. 31 which, for those friezes several metres long, implies the possession of a tool kit capable of cutting
32. 1 into limestone and the availability of enough time to carry out the decoration. Bas-reliefs only occur in sites lit by daylight (rock shelters, cave entrances); no sculpture in the strict sense (in the round, bas-relief) is known from the inner depths, which is understandable given the necessity of prolonged illumination. But the need to give the works a third dimension led to three ways of

9

1. Arcy-sur-Cure. Mammoth. Scratched lines.

achieving it: the manipulation of natural relief already mentioned; the rounding off of engraved lines; and the modelling of the paint which filled the figures. The rounding off of the inner edge of deeply engraved lines creates the effect of bas-relief, striking examples of which can be seen at
33, 34 Commarque, Les Combarelles and Font-de-Gaume: angled lighting produces a sharp relief which suggests sculpture.

PAINTING

Painting in the deep parts of caves, in the works of the richest period of the Magdalenian, develops
2 the effects of relief by different means: by filling certain parts of the body with flat colour to reflect changes in orientation of the fur; by modelling through grading a colour progressively
94, 43 from the outside to the inside (Font-de-Gaume); or by using orientated hachures for filling
78 (Niaux). At Altamira, one of the high points of Style IV, the impression of relief is created both by the use of two colours (black and red) and by clever wiping which outlined certain details and made them appear more clearly. The same process was used at Lascaux.

The search after volume was certainly not unrelated to the choice of particular natural features of the wall which could be integrated into the contour of an animal or human figure: a hollow in a wall suggesting in negative the convex relief of a rounded flank; a stalagmite constituting the sex
39 of a person; a stalactite simulating breasts (Combel); stalactite folds completed with a few lines to

10

2. Rouffignac. Mammoth and ibexes.

35 outline a bear (Tibiran), a mare (Font-de-Gaume), a bison (Castillo). Different roughnesses on the
38 wall might suggest the head of an animal: a bison (Altamira, Mas-d'Azil); a carnivore (Montespan,
36 Pergouset); an aurochs (Ebbou); a horse (Pech-Merle). The edge of a block or a fissure might
outline a bison's back (Ekaīn) or a deer's forehead (Arcy-sur-Cure). It would be interesting, for
understanding the message, to know what value was ascribed by the artist and his contemporaries
to these tricks of nature transformed into living creatures. Did their potential presence in the
folds of the cave increase the value of these drawings in relation to those of completely human
manufacture? This question does not seem to be much illuminated by an overall study of
assemblages: natural reliefs are transformed where they are found, with no evidence that they are
more important than other figures. The use of natural reliefs, the turning of the hand during the
cutting of one of the edges of an engraved line, and graphic contrivances of shading and hatching
are evidence of a pursuit of artistic research which tallies little with the accepted idea of the
palaeolithic artist, who was primitive in time but not in concepts nor in techniques.

TECHNICAL EQUIPMENT

The technical equipment of the engraver is simple. On damp walls covered with a thin skin of clay
the finger frequently sufficed to draw figures whose details were not elaborate. These 'finger lines'
are usually non-figurative in character. Elsewhere the great majority of engraved works, in fine or

11

deep engraving, were done with flint. No particular tool seems to have been assigned to the work of engraving; for example at Lascaux, below hundreds of engravings which cover the walls, flints were found with sometimes very pronounced traces of use and polish on their edges. The majority are simple waste flakes which seemed of suitable form for the job required of them.

The tool kit of the sculptor is less well known, and unfortunately no observations on the possible tools nor on the waste material from the sculpting process were made at the right time, that is during excavation. Thus even relatively recent excavations such as Mouthiers or Angles-sur-l'Anglin have produced no more scientific information than those at the beginning of the century such as at Le Roc-du-Sers or Le Cap Blanc.

The painter had recourse to different methods for applying colouring matters. These were in general made up of ochres (from yellow to red); iron oxides (limonite, haematite etc.) of different
40 hues among the more or less blackish browns; manganese dioxide for the blacks, perhaps also charcoal, but this last, exposed to the open air, disappears after a time not normally exceeding a few centuries except under exceptional conditions of preservation. According to their nature the
41 colourings were converted into powder by pounding or grinding, or were used like sticks of chalk and often trimmed like pencils. Some seem to have been hardened with an appropriate binding agent and were used like a paste to produce thick lines. Binding agents which could ensure adhesion of colouring pigments have been the subject of many suggestions (grease, blood, bone marrow etc.) which would be difficult to identify chemically after the passage of so many thousands of years. Trials seem to suggest that water, either as an added thinner or as dampness on the wall itself ensures sufficient adhesion of the pigments. One should not, however, imagine that colours were always indelibly attached to the walls; their reaction with the superficial layer of limestone sometimes resulted in disastrous variations.

The choice of instruments for the application of colour depends to an important extent on the quality of the wall, for the walls of polished marble at Niaux allow a fineness of line which the rough surfaces of other caves would not. The instruments of colour application could have been the finger of the artist himself, a stick used as a spatula, or a stick with one end mashed or crushed as the Australian aborigines still do. Real brushes of horsehair or other hair, glued or bound at one end, could have constituted true paintbrushes or stencil brushes. Lascaux provides an example of the possibilities of adaptation and the mastery of artistic processes. The first part of the cave, that of the large paintings (Hall of the Bulls and the Axial Passage) is made of walls encrusted with white calcite which could be compared to the surface of a cauliflower; the middle area (Passage) and the deepest (Apse, Nave and the Feline Gallery) are made of a limestone of medium granularity on which the application of colours is made in well-blended flat tints which do not seem to have posed any particular problems. The white calcite, on the other hand, apparently posed the Magdalenians some serious problems. The outlines were probably drawn with a paste squeezed out progressively under the thumb like a ribbon. But the filling, and even a considerable proportion of the lines, were rendered by adjoining spots a few centimetres in diameter, with fuzzy edges, which has resulted in the process being called 'spray-gun painting'. It has been supposed that the powder or paste, placed in a tubular bone, or better, a gutter-shaped one, was
42 blown on to the wall and stuck there, giving the surfaces a dappled look which, in all palaeolithic art, is unique to Lascaux (Pech-Merle is different). There are several problems with this hypothesis. The first and most obvious is that of getting the spots exactly next to each other, and

even managing to produce lines by means of successive and equidistant spots. Second, the application of blown powder to return surfaces or to ceilings is unthinkable, even without taking into account the unpleasantness of getting drops in the eyes or of swallowing ochre powder or paste. Third, it seems impossible, when one realises that more than 500 joined spots are necessary 95 for the filling of the body of the single red cow at the entrance of the Axial Passage, to imagine the painter filling his 'gutter' exactly to retain the unity of diameter of the spots, aiming to place the spots a few millimetres apart and blowing energetically to avoid too many smudges and drips at the bottom. On the several dozen painted animals in the first two parts of the cave, the few thousand spots distinguishable in the filling of the bodies and indeed in the outlines are free of such imperfections. What could have been the secret of the Lascaux painters? It seems that the artists applied the fine powder, dry or moist, on to the naturally damp wall: the instrument could have been a bundle of horsehair tied with a ligature. The same charge of powder could make two or three identical and neighbouring spots, something which can be seen on a few animals. Also, certain parts of the figure, like the lower edge of the neck, made up of joined spots, show that a light and mobile screen was used to give a clean edge to the contour. This process of using a 'mobile' stencil is shown by the fact that the spots, which would have given the edge of the neck a fuzzy and scalloped outline, are cut in a regular line by the edge of the screen.

The high technical achievement of the Lascaux artists and of those of some of the sculpted or 43 painted ensembles (Altamira, Ekaïn, Niaux, Les Trois-Frères) is obvious. It could be concluded that the technical equipment used to achieve the works that have come down to us was not inferior to that available to artists of the historic period. Flint has cutting qualities which, for work in engraving or sculpture, can rival metal tools. For the painter's materials it is the same: paintbrushes, colours in powder or pencil form, as paste or as slip, constituted materials adaptable to different categories of surface. The range of colours, from white to black, from yellows to reds and browns using the possibilities of different ochre preparations, offered very varied means of expression. This independence of artistic creation in relation to the techniques used is not the least of the characteristics of palaeolithic art: a suitable wall and a flake of flint ensured the means of self-expression as much as a piece of canvas or etching plate and a brush or a burin. Although, in spite of the surprising degree of efficiency of flint tools, the techniques of manufacture still had 15,000–20,000 years to go before reaching the present efficiency of our machines, the palaeolithic artist himself recognised from the very beginning the possibility of affirming his nature as *Homo sapiens*. If technical gesture is considered as a function parallel to the function of concrete language, among the activities possible for the hand it is the activities of artistic creation that would be the indirect evidence of the development of abstract language.

The freedom to create forms can perhaps be demonstrated in another way. One can wonder about the influence of the process on the style of the art. Many examples, taken either from works in the same style but different in technique (Covalanas, Ebbou, La Pasiega) or from those in the same technique but different in style (Lascaux, Rouffignac), show that the manner of painting with continuous or punctuated lines, or of sketching, has no obvious influence on the quality of the curve any more than the nature of the surface which only influenced the choice of process. These facts indicate that, from the Upper Solutrean at least, the mastery of different processes was advanced enough for the characteristics of style not to be influenced by technique to any great extent.

It is not easy to mould language, an essentially linear process, to the expression of the many dimensions of visual perception. If one wants to express the stylistic properties of a prehistoric work of art, one often adopts an indirect method, whose means are akin to poetry and involve value judgements. The observer's attention is attracted by a qualitative description which allows him to pursue the reconstruction of the image that one wishes to communicate to him by drawing on his personal store of images without using the channel of words. This means that one can only put into the comprehension of works of art that which one can personally bring to them. This is why it has seemed preferable to seek out an objective, analytical and direct way which must then necessarily use language without an evocative bias. This serves to multiply the ways and means for trying to demonstrate the multiple dimensions of the figurative phenomenon.

Form

It is difficult to create a vocabulary of forms, especially if it is hoped to encompass all cases throughout all time and across the whole world. It is, however, essential to use discrete units to describe forms in a most general way so that a total or partial influence of form on style can perhaps be detected. It is to this end that we propose a morphological framework capable of bringing to parietal and rupestral art in particular the elements of a first-stage classification. This is in the form of a progressive scale based on *figurative states*. Developed out of research on African, American and Oceanic sculpture, and adapted to works on a parietal support, this analytical device comprises four morphologically successive levels without implying the direction in which the transition is made from one level to another. As experience suggests, artistic evolution does not accumulate its innovations in the same way as, for example, manufacturing techniques. The four levels or figurative states are: pure geometric, geometric figurative, synthetic figurative and analytical figurative. The linking properties of the different segments which constitute the figure can be defined as *elementary* (e.g. elementary synthetic figurative): concise lines, threadlike, amoeba-like; or *with juxtaposed elements*: grouping of segments by abrupt cuts from one to the next; or *with linked elements*: grouping by fused joins.

PURE GEOMETRIC

Groups of lines constituting geometric figures, unidentifiable because of an absence of oral or written context, are as numerous in palaeolithic art as they are in art of later periods. From the Mousterian (*c.* 60,000 BC) up to the appearance of identifiable drawings during the prefigurative period, only rare examples are known, fragments of bone with straight lines or confused curves.

GEOMETRIC FIGURATIVE

Geometric lines or areas whose grouping allows at least the relative identification of the subject. In palaeolithic parietal art the pure geometric and the geometric figurative only affect the signs,

15

while the animal figures, in contrast, show a development in form towards a more and more
44–47 precise analysis. This geometricisation of the signs in contrast with the character of the animal figures is one of the interesting aspects of research into the meaning of the designs. The examples of geometric and geometric figurative are much more numerous in mobiliary art than in parietal art. In fact, certain categories of decorated objects, in particular spear points and generally objects with a short life, carry signs which correspond to the geometricisation of animal figures: reindeer or ibex heads seen from the front and reduced to four 'brackets' of which two represent
3 the horns and two the ears – or a row of horses reduced to a line of saw teeth. These geometric figurative elements create a context which allows the identification of figures that might not be there just on their own account. This important question will be taken up again later (see *abbreviation*).

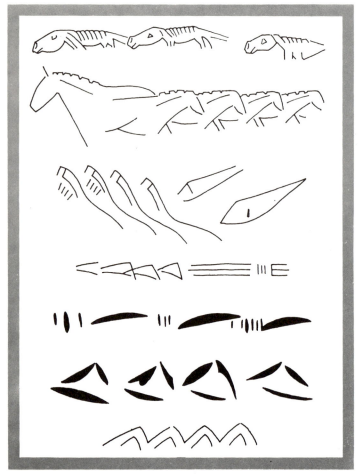

3. The evolution of decoration on objects leads in two different directions: the progressive development of precision in the whole and the detail of decoration which involves objects whose precarious nature is irrelevant, either because of their character as objects of long usage or because for various reasons the figures on bone or stone plaques are represented by figures rendered 'photographically'. The second direction corresponds to geometricisation by the reduction of the figure to its principal traits. Once involved in this, another world is opened up leading to abbreviated symbols which come close to elements of ideographic character.

SYNTHETIC FIGURATIVE

The lines express the essentials of the form of the subject without representing the fine detail of the contours seen by the eye. It is often noticeable that details of identification like antlers, horns, ears, dewlap, tail are in a different state from other parts of the body, particularly the extremities. The synthetic figurative marks, in all arts, the most dynamic stages between the geometric which tends towards the non-figurative, and the analytical which reaches visual accuracy. Taking figures which in all cases could have marked for their period a notable regression or advance, it seems that we possess enough coherent elements to consider that from the Aurignacian to the beginning of the Magdalenian (30,000–13,000 BC), palaeolithic art passed through different figurative stages 45 from geometric figurative (Cellier shelter) to synthetic figurative with juxtaposed elements 81. 31 (Pech-Merle, early phase) or to synthetic figurative with linked elements (Ebbou). This 5. 48. 49 progression confirms and makes precise, on a technical basis, the character and limits of Styles I, II, III and IV proposed in 1965. Lascaux, at the boundary of synthetic figurative with juxtaposed elements and analytical figurative with linked elements, bears witness to an evolution leading from archaism to the first forms of classicism, of which Altamira, in the following stage, will be the example.

4. Las Chimeneas. Stag. Very synthetic representation.

5. La Baume Latrone. Proboscid, probably a mammoth.

ANALYTICAL FIGURATIVE ·

Characterised by research into visual reality, through an execution shaded by the modulation of lines and by proportions, the analytical figurative tends towards a total representation of the anatomically natural morphology. Analytical works correspond in the groupings with Style IV, 6. 52 and are characteristic of Middle and Upper Magdalenian: Altamira, Ekaîn, Las Monedas for Spain; 53 Niaux, Font-de-Gaume, Les Combarelles, Rouffignac, Teyjat for France; Levanzo for Italy, offer good examples of what could be considered as the 'classic' period of palaeolithic cave art.

The figurative states in no way ensure a complete coverage of all the variations in figurative expression. We still have to bring in the very important aspects associated with spatial integration (superimposition, framing, perspective) and temporal integration (animation) if we are to try to construct a model characterising the evolution of palaeolithic art. This evolution progressed over

17

20,000 years on a trajectory leading from the elementary synthetic figurative towards a more and more precise analysis of form, the trajectory being not unlike that followed by certain art styles considered as classic, such as Greek art between the Bronze Age and Hellenistic periods.

It is useful not to lose sight of the fact that the most obvious questions, those related to notions of time and space, are posed by assemblages like Lascaux, Niaux and Altamira which are in a position high up in the figurative states. We should also note that post-glacial works, like the petroglyphs from the Alps (Mont Bego, Val Camonica) or Iberia are descended neither in form nor in the expression of volume from palaeolithic works. Most of them are at the first stages on the figurative scale (geometric or synthetic figurative), which well illustrates the contrast between the evolution of material culture, in which technical progress is the inheritance of chronologically successive societies, and the evolution of the figurative arts, which does not reflect the development of technical abilities but of socio-economic states. In one form or another the relationships of artistic creation with global society are linked to the chronological relationships between figuration and activities essential for living. Palaeolithic figurative art, because of its extraordinary longevity (what other art could notch up 20,000 years of continuous evolution?), is also evidence of the extraordinary stability of the relationships between society, its resources, and the artistic practitioner.

6. Ekaïn. Horse.

Space

Because of the long dominant theory of the chance nature of the distribution of parietal figures, few authors have approached the problem of the representation of space in palaeolithic art. The subject is treated here in the strictly technical sense, taking into account the nature of usable surfaces, lighting and the conditions of movement for the artist. The variety of situations between narrow tunnels, where the work could only have been carried out by lying on the ground, and the vast vaults of certain caves suits well an exposition of the principles of representation of space.

JUXTAPOSITION AND SUPERIMPOSITION

It seems convenient, and in many cases appropriate, to start from the idea of the *manual field*, defined as the area accessible to the artist without changing position. The validity of this idea is confirmed by the fact that about 70% of wall paintings are between 25 and 80 cm in maximum diameter, suggesting a manual field with radius of 30 to 40 cm. Three types of spatial organisation for the figures can be proposed: *figures widely juxtaposed*, where the distance between them is variable but is greater than the average length of the animals represented; *figures closely juxtaposed*, where the distance between them is less than the average length; and *superimposed figures*, where drawing them on the same surface imposes at least partial overlapping. These different spatial dispositions involve figures belonging to the same panel, that is to the surface of a wall with limits defined by the shape of the cave.

Juxtaposition

Figures in wide or close juxtaposition correspond to a mode of representation common to numerous art styles from all periods. This mode reflects a stage in the evolution of graphical expression where the problems of representing perspective by overlapping have not been mastered, or a form of expression which deals with the representation of space in a different way. Lascaux has a number of examples of heads or tails in strange positions with the sole purpose, apparently, of avoiding the rump or head of a neighbouring figure. Juxtaposition is distinctive of the majority of palaeolithic assemblages.

Superimposition

54   The result of an attitude apparently contradictory to that concerned with juxtaposition, is a complex phenomenon which in one of its aspects (simultaneous superimposition) has hardly any equivalent in other art styles. Prehistorians have seen in it a true stratification, of the same order as the chronological stratigraphy of the geologists, and have felt it necessary to establish the order of succession of different figures, believing them to have been created at different times. A sequence does exist, but it does not presume the length of time that has passed between the two or three engraved or painted lines at issue, which could as well have been a few minutes as several centuries or millennia. We are indebted to A. Laming-Emperaire (1957) for raising the question of intentional and significant superimposition. In mobiliary art on plaques or blocks we often find several figures engraved on top of one another (La Colombière, Limeuil): it is impossible to envisage a long period of time between the execution of the different images. It is nevertheless necessary to set aside cases where figures of genuinely different periods are superimposed on one wall, but these cases are rather rare. Three categories can be proposed: diachronic super-impositions, additions and restorations, and partial overlapping.

Diachronic superimpositions have for a long time helped to cherish the illusion that a parietal stratigraphy existed through which different phases of superimposed figures would be revealed (Cartailhac, Breuil, Glory). It now appears that not only is it often impossible to distinguish the real succession of superimposed lines (micro-alterations of pigment) but also that one could search in vain for a sufficient number of cases on which to base a chronological certainty (Ebbou). It could almost be regarded as a law that subsequent palaeolithic people placed their drawings beside earlier ones or in another place (La Mouthe).

Additions and restorations are relatively rare, but in the case of paintings this may be because of the present state of the pigments which hardly allows such distinctions to be made. The paintings with engravings either underneath or on top (Altamira, Lascaux) are evidence of purely technical processes, the engraving occurring on the one hand as a location device and on the other as a livening-up of the painted surface. It is at Lascaux that retouching is most visible, for numerous painted or engraved figures have been renovated (horses whose ear positions or stags whose antlers have been corrected to a perspective more in line with optical reality). But it is in bas-relief that reworkings are perhaps most obvious. At those sites most eminent in respect of their

55, 56   sculpture (Angles-sur-l'Anglin, Cap Blanc, Mouthiers, Roc-du-Sers) careful examination of the reliefs reveals reworkings of sometimes great significance: horses changed into bisons or vice versa. The motives for these transformations, which must have been carried out several years or centuries, rather than several millennia, later are totally enigmatic.

Partial overlapping would have been more in place among the different processes of perspective had it not been, for nearly three-quarters of a century, the object of a confusion. In fact, when

Cartailhac and Breuil formulated the theory of 'parietal stratigraphy', they took, as an example thought to be convincing, two bisons from Marsoulas. But one complete bison seems to cover the body of a second with only the head visible beyond the rump of the first, while the horns of a third apparently suggest the superimposition of three figures. Fitting in to the ideas of a period which had not yet considered groups of figures to be significant assemblages, the ensemble looks like good proof of the spacing out in time of figures occupying walls by chance. It is surprising that it was not noticed that not only were the three bison heads of the same manufacture, which deprives the stratigraphy of a good part of its interest, but also that a border with no paint applied distinctly separates the rump of the first bison from the neck of the one which seemed to be covered. We are dealing here not with figures which would have been drawn partly overlapping in two different periods, but with synchronous figures where the painting is interrupted at the outline of one of them. The figures thus appear to be slid one beneath the other, and the part which would have been painted over remains in reserve.

Lascaux offers the most remarkable examples of this technique, in particular the horse between the two confronting aurochs in the Hall of the Bulls, or the large black bull in the Axial Passage which effectively covers two cows, but whose cervico-dorsal line is bristling with several horns whose outlines stop at the back of the animal. Partial overlapping could, in fact, be regarded either as a way of drawing perspective, or rather as a device to avoid encroachment of one figure on another.

Transparency, a process which consists in drawing the organs within the outline of an animal as if seen in X-ray, has sometimes been mentioned in relation to the superimposition of palaeolithic figures. This figurative mode exists in contemporary Australian painting and also in the rupestral art of Scandinavia, Siberia and India. Although it has been mentioned in relation to several superimpositions like those of horses 8 and 9 on the panel of the 'emblazoned cow' in the Nave at Lascaux, it is totally absent from palaeolithic cave art, and the examples claimed are the subject of errors in interpretation.

Simultaneous superimpositions: a significant proportion of the cases of superimposition seems to reflect a particular attitude of the palaeolithic artist regarding figurative space; as if there existed for him an extended space where figures are juxtaposed, and a condensed space where they are superimposed. Such an attitude, even if it reflects purely practical constraints, would offer great interest for the understanding of figural assemblages, the artist having the choice of superimposing several figures whose grouping was significant rather than drawing them at a greater distance from one another. The cases of intensive superimposition concern engraving in particular and are situated for the most part in low narrow caves (Les Combarelles) or in recesses of limited size (Font-de-Gaume, 'Chamber of the small bisons'; Gargas, 'La Conque'; Pech-Merle, 'Le Combel'; Les Trois-Frères, the Sanctuary). In all these cases the limits of the manual field caused by the dimensions of the surface or the physical situation of the artist are obvious. The limitation of field seems to be just as constraining for the plaques in mobiliary art (La Colombière).

The dimensions and configuration of the support are not enough to explain multiple superimpositions, for one could wonder why the artist did not reduce the size of the figures in order to juxtapose them, as in numerous art traditions, rupestral or not, ancient or modern.

21

Different hypotheses can be formulated, two of which are of special interest. The first arises from a negative argument: except in a few very rare cases (the scene in the Lascaux Shaft), groups of figures in palaeolithic art are not narrative in character. Although a hunting scene demands the juxtaposition of hunter and game to be intelligible, the absence of pictographic care renders the superimposition of the participants immaterial. The second and complementary hypothesis is that reasons could have existed for grouping the subjects. This positive attitude is difficult to prove completely, and it must have varied in different times and places, but enough examples exist for the question to remain interesting. The large black bull in the Axial Passage at Lascaux, apart from the half-dozen horns in red ochre which bristle along its dorsal line, is superimposed on two bovine figures (apparently cows). The whole thing could be seen as a repainting of the parietal decoration, but it cannot be ruled out that we are looking at the telescoping of figures whose

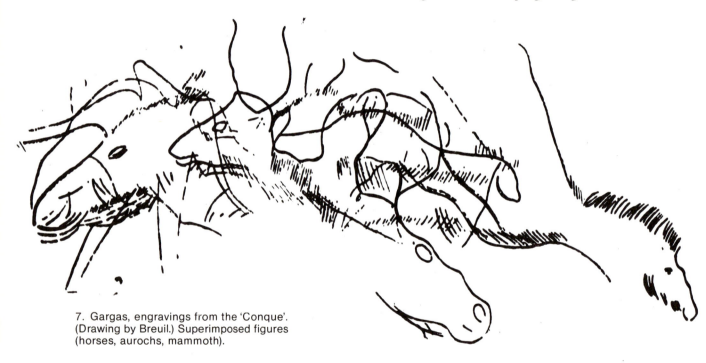

7. Gargas, engravings from the 'Conque'. (Drawing by Breuil.) Superimposed figures (horses, aurochs, mammoth).

association would be significant. The black frieze from Pech-Merle is another fairly impressive example. The large panel consists of two groups of paintings, one comprising aurochs, mammoths and horses and the other bisons, mammoths and a horse. The main group is the bison–horse group which occupies the centre of a panel some six metres long. The left hand part of the ensemble contains, in two metres, the figures of the first group with only one case of partial superimposition, a return in the wall allowing the placing of almost all the figures in close juxtaposition. The central group, in contrast, consists of a horse and two bisons whose size overshoots the four metres of available wall; and the three animals are not only superimposed on one another but also on some of the mammoths which occupy the lower border of the panel. This large panel is extended over ten more metres by an irregular wall, with surfaces of modest dimensions separated by faults or crevices. Five bison–mammoth groups follow one another on the usable surfaces; their size is a function of the available surface, but all the pairs of figures are widely juxtaposed. Consequently in this frieze, whose unity of composition is the proof of a coherent assemblage, we find evidence for the flexibility of the process of mythographic assemblage: the representation of the different protagonists takes precedence over the legibility of the images.

A more curious case can be seen on panel III of the 'Salon Noir' at Niaux. The basic assemblage is horse–bison–ibex, which is found in each of the four panels making up the whole. Panel III is particularly striking: numerous little figures are in close juxtaposition, notably the little horse 1 in relation to bison 2, the little ibex 3 in relation to horse 4, while horse 5 is superimposed on the crupper of bison 2 and the vertical bison 6 is superimposed on the crupper of horse 4. These

8. Les Combarelles assemblage 69.6.
Horses, bison, mammoth.

different examples suggest that superimposition can be synchronically imposed, being perceived as a specific form of representation. This suggestion points to a mental step of the artist, a very important step which is that of the framing of figures in relation to available surfaces.

FRAMING

It has emerged from the study of numerous figures from both mobiliary and parietal art that they present the same characteristics of framing. On mobiliary plaques as well as on decorated walls it seems that single figures, or the first figure of a series of jumbled figures, correspond to the maximum utilisation of the available field (vertical diameter, horizontal, or both); that is to say that the artist mentally located the image he wanted in the largest available area of the support. The procedure began with the head, which dictated the other proportions: on an equal surface a deer, because of its antlers, is drawn smaller than a horse superimposed upon it. The part of the surface opposite the head may remain empty (Limeuil). In cave art, examples of fitting in to the maximum available diameters are very numerous. This phenomenon plays an important role in the integration of figures into the natural form of the support. It is a principal element in the feeling of grandeur which one experiences in front of the works. Superimposition and framing are closely linked, and complementary, the artist manipulating to the full the features of the support. In fact, if superimposition can be related to the significance of the grouping of figures, the principal motives are of a technical and psychological character; they comply with the demands of the manual field and of framing, demands which in palaeolithic art are not reduced or inhibited by the necessity of a descriptive organisation, as they are in a number of later art styles.

SYMMETRY

Research into the possible practice of symmetry in palaeolithic art might seem to be fruitless. In fact, the first impression left by cave art, in which animals in profile predominate and in which the large assemblages of animals seem to be arranged in a disorderly manner, is that symmetry is

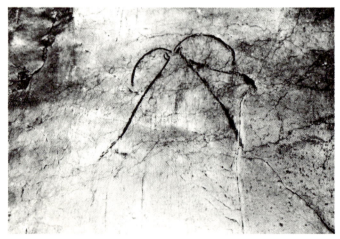

9. Niaux. Ibexes.

completely absent. The word does not even figure in the work by S. Giedion, who is one of the rare authors to have approached the concept of palaeolithic space (*The eternal present*, New York 1962). However, three types of symmetry can be distinguished, represented by a varying number of examples: mirror symmetry, symmetry of mass and oblique symmetry.

Mirror symmetry, in which the two halves of the subject or the series of subjects are repeated in inverted positions, is the least common form of symmetry in the Palaeolithic, even though there are numerous signs whose construction is rigorously symmetrical. Living creatures seen face-on are rare: human faces (Combarelles, Marsoulas), horse (Lascaux), feline (Trois-Frères). Still less common are symmetrical assemblages, but they are highly significant. In fact they all fall into the category of opposed animals, depicting natural behaviour. It is a question of conditioned symmetry, of a process of description rather than of construction. Of this nature are the crossed bisons at Lascaux, the confronted ibex at Roc-du-Sers, Lascaux and Niaux, and the confronting mammoths at Rouffignac. The behaviour of confrontation creates an axis of symmetry which normally only involves two animals but which, at Rouffignac, seems to have entailed the drawing of two confronting herds.

Symmetry of mass corresponds to a device in which the two opposed halves, different in subject-matter but of a roughly equivalent mass, balance each other in relation to the axis of symmetry. Palaeolithic examples of this construction are relatively numerous: one of the most striking is that in the Passage of the Signs in El Castillo (Breuil's Group 23), which occupies the right-hand wall of the passage, one near the entrance and the other near the far end. The first is made up of two quadrilateral signs arranged in a cross, the second of two quadruple rows of dots also arranged in a cross. This layout of two groups of different signs quite close in their outline, unique in palaeolithic parietal art, looks like a spontaneous essay in symmetry.

Animal figures also offer several examples: the large confronting bulls at Lascaux; the two elongated women, one accompanied by a bison and the other by a horse, at La Magdelaine; the bison and the horse, each of which occupies one side of the chamber, at Marcenac; and the reindeer and the horse, each placed on one side of a dihedron, at Las Monedas. If it must be said of mirror symmetry that it is not a matter of composition but rather that it depicts animal behaviour, this is not so in the case of the symmetry of mass. Here it is difficult not to see a deliberate intention, or at least a more or less conscious perception of a material balance applicable to an intellectually significant assemblage, even if the artist was using to best advantage the favourable conditions of the support.

Oblique symmetry appears as a formula for grouping in a fair number of cases, which are to be found among the most remarkable of the parietal ensembles. Oblique symmetry here should be understood as the spatial organisation of figures whose homologous points are distributed according to parallel obliques on either side of the axis of symmetry. At several sites (Cougnac, Altamira, Pech-Merle) there are paired figures (male and female ibexes, male ibexes following each other, bison and mammoth) partially overlapping and arranged along an oblique line. This composition offers numerous variations in which analogous figures are grouped in pairs on an oblique axis (group 8 hands at Gargas, 'dappled' horses at Pech-Merle, bisons 'at bay' at Lascaux).

25

This kind of spatial integration can be found in a more complex form, in which two groups of animals cross each other (with or without partial overlapping) following an oblique axis of symmetry. We find this sort of assemblage very early (25,000 BC) (Pair-non-Pair) and we can discern its presence until the best Magdalenian sites (Niaux, Santimamiñe) (12,000–9000BC). Oblique symmetry is associated with framing and superimposition, and also with the expression of perspective. This subject is discussed again a little later and is limited here to a few examples. Panel I of the 'Salon Noir' at Niaux has six bisons in two groups of three which interrelate in a unit on one side and the other of the axis of symmetry, the group on the right facing left and the left-hand group facing right. The same tendency towards an oblique arrangement is seen among the other 'Salon Noir' panels, particularly in Panel III where the horses (all but one facing right), albeit different in scale (certainly significant), occupy the lower part of the assemblage while the bisons (two facing right, four facing left) are distributed in the upper half in a device similar to that of the Panel I bisons. It should also be noted that horses 4 and 5 demonstrate between them the same spatial relationship as the horses in the neighbouring Panel IV. If, through simple caution, it is impossible to be certain that we are in the presence of true composition, or even that the artist (or artists) was expressing the rules of an organised method, the spatial relationships between the figures are sufficiently close-knit to correspond with a certain awareness of artistic construction. It seems that, apart from the signs, symmetry was in some way accidental. It appears rather as one of the spontaneous solutions to the balancing of groups of figures. Natural circumstances (the confrontation of mammoths or ibexes) facilitate its appearance. However, among the examples of oblique symmetry (Pech-Merle horses, Panel I at Niaux, the large panel at Ekaīn) there exists the probability of at least the awareness of a rhythmically balanced composition even if not a conscious search for the symmetry of figures.

REPRESENTATION OF THE GROUND-SURFACE

Framing and symmetry establish a first approach to the palaeolithic imagination (imagination taken in the strict sense of the ability to create images). One may wonder about the creation of the illusion of space and about the relationships between the figures and the walls which bear them. We saw above that irregularities in the wall were frequently used to give volume to animals or men – concavity used to advantage to simulate the convexity of a flank, stalactites suggesting feet, a stalagmitic column suggesting the sex of a human figure – but the support here only plays the part of an element of body mass. So it is interesting to see what role can be played by the support seen as the ground surface. The representation of the ground can be summarised under three headings: undefined ground-surface, linear ground-surface and ground-surface in perspective.

Undefined ground-surface. In many examples the relationship between the extremities of the limbs and the support is not clarified. A common occurrence, particularly in the early styles is that the extremities of the limbs are simply eliminated (for example at Ebbou). It is also common in the later styles, where a significant proportion of the figures have no feet. The missing section of the limbs is of varying importance; sometimes limited to the foot itself, it can extend to the level of the chest or thighs.

There is a second version of the undefined ground-surface where juxtaposed or superimposed figures do not have levels in common nor any indication of individual levels (Pech-Merle: centre of the Black Frieze; Le Portel: the 'Camarin'; Niaux: the assemblage on clay; Ekaïn: bear).

Linear ground-surface. Figures showing the existence of a relationship between the animal and the ground are very common. This ground-surface is never shown by engraving or painting, or at least we know of no examples. On the contrary, it commonly takes one of the two following forms: the imaginary line or the natural line.

The imaginary ground-surface line appears when at least two animals are following or confronting one another in such a way that their extremities (drawn or not) can be found on the same imaginary line. Rouffignac has two particularly convincing examples: the three rhinoceroses following one another and the frieze of 11 mammoths, in two groups and confronting each other. In the same cave one can come across figures corresponding to different relationships with the support, as at Pair-non-Pair where, among the figures superimposed or juxtaposed without defined ground-surface, there are two horses in a line and two confronting bovines which fall into the category of figures on an imaginary ground-surface. Pair-non-Pair is one of the earliest parietal assemblages, and this evidence shows that the process of suggesting the linear ground-surface through the relationship of two animals is early, since it goes back to Style II (about 25,000 BC).

Similar assemblages are to be found at Cougnac (frieze of the three megaceros), at La Dérouine (2 horses, a mammoth), at Teyjat (two cows and a bull, two bisons). This last site shows that the same process lasted until the end of the Magdalenian at around 9000 BC. Parietal Italian art, which must be virtually contemporary, contains several assemblages of aurochs, equids or bucks in pairs resting on an imaginary ground surface. The best example is that of the famous panel in the cave of the Adduara: human and animal figures suggest a ground-surface on which they move about in different directions.

The natural ground-surface line is a response to the same sort of idea but by the inverse procedure: the ground-surface line is not created by the alignment of the figures, but the figures (single or multiple) seem to stand on a ground-surface line created by a fissure, the edge of a wall, a ledge, a stratification joint, all perceptibly horizontal. Occasionally the natural feature which provides the image of the linear ground-surface is inclined in relation to the horizontal and, without altering their bodily attitude, the animals follow the inclination of the ground-surface line. One example,

10. Rouffignac. Line of three rhinoceroses.

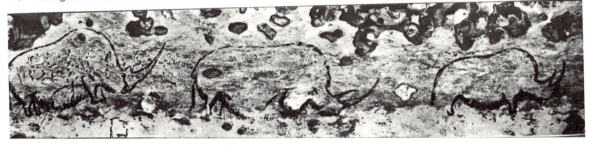

27

66   from Le Portel is the horse in Gallery 2 whose image follows a stratification joint inclined at about 30°. Another example, at El Castillo, is provided by two bisons in a row appearing to descend a similar slope constituted by a ledge. The most unusual of the relationships between image and support is given by the three bisons of Santimamiñe, painted vertically on ground-surface lines made up of the folds of a stalactite drapery 90° from the horizontal (see below: animals in unusual positions).

Ground-surface in linear perspective. Was the Magdalenian artist conscious enough of real space to consider parietal space as a symbolic image of it? The total absence of figures which could correspond to vegetable or mineral images means we cannot speak of 'landscape'; and there are many other art styles which have not needed to represent the ground-surface, implying its presence by using the levels of animal and human figures and by their partial overlapping. Palaeolithic men knew both processes, and this inspires one to investigate up to what point the parietal surfaces, like the figures themselves, were perceived as something other than a support – as an area to which one could confer a third dimension through perspective. Before approaching what we can learn of perspective, there remains one important point: figures in unusual positions.

ANIMALS IN UNUSUAL POSITIONS

Whether or not they stand on an imaginary or natural ground-surface, the majority of animals are represented in a normal stance, the body roughly horizontal and the limbs not varying from the vertical except in physically normal ways. But a proportion of figures depart from the normal attitude and are presented vertically or even upside down. This unusual position can be explained in several ways. First, it could stem from the situation or the nature of the support: framing could have made use of ground-surface lines which tempted the painter (Santimamiñe, stalactite), and the fissures or vertical joints could also have inspired him to set the figure on end in order to take

68   advantage of a wider field (Altxerri). Second, the support could be in such a position that the orientation of the figures did not matter: the engraved plaques of stalagmite from Teyjat, clearly horizontal, were decorated with figures executed from different sides which were superimposed across each other. The same effect is produced with ceiling surfaces. Third, while the two preceding situations involve the support, and can concern both groups of animals and isolated figures, this suggestion is concerned more particularly with grouped animals among which one or

119   two (rarely more than two) are drawn in a position perpendicular to that of the majority in the panel. If the ensemble is considered to represent a herd in slow progression, at pasture, such as it would appear to a hunter, the majority of animals face in the same direction, generally backs to the wind, but among them some occupy perpendicular positions. The panels of bisons at La Mouthe, Niaux, Altamira and Santimamiñe are of this kind. Amongst the figures in unusual positions, animated examples are rare: apart from the 'rolling' bisons from Altamira, one can cite the little rearing horse in the Black Cow group in the Nave at Lascaux, the wounded bison with bent legs from Niaux, the upturned horse in the Axial Passage at Lascaux, the 'falling' aurochs in the Black Frieze at Pech-Merle and the perpendicular head of the first horse in the 'hunting scene' at Montespan. All these figures seem to have an anecdotal rather than a metaphysical character. Of the three solutions proposed, the framing and the narrative representation (herd or animated

individual) seem to be the most likely. We must also take note of the fact that among the 57 recognised drawings of vertical animals, 36 are bisons and only 6 are horses. For animals upside-down the figures are reversed, for of 5 noted examples 4 are horses. Among the other possible subjects only rare individuals of hind and ibex are represented. If it is noted that collective behaviour is different for different species, it could be supposed that there is an ethological connotation for these figures in unusual positions. One approach, if not for all of the animals in groups, would testify to the existence of a 'flattened perspective' on the field of a support consciously perceived as a ground-surface.

PERSPECTIVE

The expression of the third spatial dimension can be achieved by different processes. The most simple is that of partial overlapping. We have seen that total or partial superimposition can result from the matching of the support with the mental images of the artist who used the largest area possible. Similarly we have seen that when the representation of several animals is undertaken, juxtaposition may also be involved in certain cases (Lascaux, tail of the horse in the Axial Passage,

11 Mas-d'Azil. Animals superimposed.

horses' heads in the 'Empreinte' and the Nave). Such cases relate to the image of the animal whose figure takes precedence in the space, in the nature of a support for a group of juxtaposed figures; the space here is simply the interval between figures which, as we shall see, can be individually in
11 perspective. There is thus reason to consider the possibility of the existence of a perspective based on the partial overlapping of figures. But it seems straightway impossible to include all the examples of partial superimpositions in a study of volume, since a number of them fall into the category of superimposition in its real sense (see above). The numerous superimpositions on the walls of Pair-non-Pair are clearly not attempts to portray perspective: the Style II animals jumbled up there do not constitute assemblages which can be included as partial overlapping. Similarly at

7   Gargas, the very large number of Style II and early Style III figures abound there in superimpositions which simply reflect the limitations of the figurative field.

If we refer to the example of Lascaux, there are numerous cases where the engraving of a whole animal is superimposed by several other animals with no more links with perspective than at Pair-non-Pair and Gargas. But among the paintings there are several about which one might pose the question. The first of the aurochs facing right in the Hall of the Bulls is partly covered by a large horse, which in turn is partly covered by a small horse whose haunches rest on the ledge in the wall.

57   In front of the horns of the bull which faces the above there can also be seen a large horse limited to the head, the neck and the back. A cow in the Axial Passage has the same parts defined by a fuzzy edge which shows the animal going behind the silhouette of a small horse. But do such examples reflect a real perspective? The whole drawing of the horse in the Hall of the Bulls should have obliterated the head of the first aurochs and at least two of the small deer; the drawing of the cow should have hidden the small horse and the head of the large red cow at the entrance to the Axial Passage. These different examples therefore do not help to resolve the problem of perspective achieved by partial overlapping. They rather tend to prove the contrary: juxtaposition and not superimposition is demonstrated, by the process of blurring which allows the evocation of a form without imposing on it harsh outlines. Here it is a case of a device of framing, the evidence for the high symbolic dominance of the images some 13,000 years BC.

The test may be carried out in another way. Realistic themes are not common in palaeolithic art; generally animals do not behave in a very active manner, and their representation is only rarely coordinated with that of their neighbours. There is, however, an aspect of animation that is of great interest, that of the two male bisons with feet crossing as if in defiance at the time of a rut.

85   This scene is repeated four times at Lascaux a few metres apart. This aspect will be discussed again when looking at the idea of time in palaeolithic symbolism, but because the two animals cross, the space which marks their meeting does correspond to a perspective, with one animal close and another less so. It must be added to this that the four assemblages do not correspond in terms of time, for the two in the Apse cross at head to tail, those on the Panel of the Empreinte a little further, those in the Passage of the Felines at head to shoulders, and those of the famous group of the 'bisons at bay' in the Nave at crupper to crupper.

Perpendiculars express the relationships of limbs to the support, whether it be a ground-surface line or a surface without a particular feature. These relationships affect the manner in which the link between the limb and the body is made, and in particular the way in which extremities are treated. In fact, an evolution is perceptible in the way in which foot is in contact with ground. The absence of feet is common in figures of all periods, but there is sufficient evidence to suggest the following

72   evolution of horse's hooves: 'ball-like' hooves at Le Roc-du-Sers, Lascaux and Le Gabillou, and hooves truly drawn in perspective as if seen from the height of a man, on the horses of the 'Salon Noir' at Niaux. The same sequence can be suggested for bisons, whose hooves, oval and divided

73   into two equal halves at Altamira and Lascaux, become visually correct at Niaux, Santimamiñe and Marsoulas where the perpendiculars establish a relationship with the support, to rise from a vertical surface, so as to convey the impression of horizontal space.

Perpendiculars assist with another consideration: when feet are standing on a ground-surface
70   line or on an imaginary surface, normally the four limbs ought to be of unequal length in lateral
      pairs, those nearest the observer being longer than the two on the opposite side. This
71   arrangement represents the polygon of sustentation. This optical necessity does not seem to have
78   preoccupied palaeolithic man, for all formulas can be found: the four limbs can be the same
      length, which reduces the polygon of sustentation to a line, or the four limbs can be of unequal
      length, or the front and back legs can be inverted in their arrangement which, from the geometric
      point of view, is rather disconcerting. But the great majority fall into the categories of limbs of
      equal length or unfinished limbs; only a minority of Middle or Late Magdalenian figures have
      limbs with the correct perpendiculars.

TERMINOLOGICAL OBSERVATIONS ON PERSPECTIVE

The representation of space in living or recent art has only been the subject of a small number of
studies, except for the art of the great civilisations. This is all the more true of the study of
prehistoric parietal art, for which we only have the rare studies of G.H. Luquet (1930), Raphael
(1945), Giedion (1957), and the reflections scattered throughout the Abbé Breuil's works.
Perspective is only mentioned incidentally in these works, and only on detailed points. The
optical convention which consists of creating the illusion of three-dimensional space on a two-
dimensional surface by means of lines of flight was established slowly in western cultures, and
without eliminating other forms of representation of space like *cavalier perspective, superimposition* or
partial overlapping, *juxtaposition* and *perspective by flattening*, in which the subjects seem to be lying
on the ground. Flattened perspective may also lead to the representation of parts of the subject
which cannot be seen from the angle of the observer. Between these different forms of
conventional representation of space there is a progression from abstract comprehension
(Luquet's intellectual realism) of the subject, through the multiplicity of approaches to optical
structuring (linear perspective). If, for comparison, one takes the evidence of the drawing activity
of children and adults in different cultures in historical time, one can perceive the progressive
subjugation of abstract perception by a logically technical process: the vision of the subject
starting from a unique viewpoint.

This evolution which, bar historical accident, will lead from *intellectual realism* to *optical realism*,
expresses a phenomenon comparable to that revealed by the 'figurative states', that is a process of
technical maturation. The two series of terms define two aspects of the same approach to
76   figurative creation. The La Grèze bison is at the same time in synthetic figurative and, for the
      horns, in flattened perspective (bi-angular direct perspective). The Niaux or Santimamiñe bisons
74   are in analytical figurative and in optical perspective (uni-angular perspective). These two
      observations can already be used as a first step towards a definition of style.

Juxtaposition, partial superimposition and perpendiculars ensure on their side a grasp of the
collective aspects of perspective, that is to say of the assemblages of figures capable of belonging
to the same surface and constituting a homogeneous and significant grouping. The word

'perspective' has been used by prehistorians, particularly when talking about horns and antlers, but it has not been invoked in the description of relationships between figures in the same assemblage. Prehistorians have presumed for a long time that since the figures were executed one by one over many millennia by different painters or engravers, no figurative links between them could have been intended. The fact of denying the possibility of the representation of groups of animals rather than of isolated individuals at Altamira or Niaux is all the more curious because the same authors have admitted the existence of herds of bovines in African parietal art without raising the slightest discussion. Both are in analytical figurative and most frequently in perspective by partial superimposition or by juxtaposition, but the most obvious difference between the Franco-Hispanic palaeolithic assemblages and the African ones is concerned with animation (see later), and above all with the characteristic of mythographic space of the former compared with the pictographic space of the latter.

In respect of individual figures the principal difficulty arises from the lack of a simple but precise definition of the relationships in space of the component parts. As for the 'figurative states', it has seemed necessary to give an extended terminology, arising from other art styles but adapted to the special needs of the study of palaeolithic art. This is why we suggest the application of the following formulas.

A *Simple profile:* stage zero of perspective. The subject is seen as an infinity of points situated on a line which would be parallel to it. Pair-non-Pair engravings, La Grèze bison, La Baume Latrone paintings.

B *Bi- or multi-angular opposed perspective.* The different parts of the subject can be flattened out through 180°. It is the maximum extent of 'intellectual realism', since the subject can be seen from four sides at the same time. There are no Palaeolithic examples, but there is some evidence in post-glacial art (Mont Bego, etc.).

C *Bi-angular direct perspective.* The subject is viewed alternately from the front and in profile, and the different parts can be flattened out through 90°: a man with a front-facing body and a head in profile, or a bison with a body in profile and the horns from the front. This is Breuil's 'twisted perspective'. This convention for perspective is common to many historic, protohistoric and prehistoric arts (Egyptian art, etc.) and to a certain stage in the drawings of children. It complies with the rule of the *most explicit line*, each part of the subject being seen from the angle at which it is most easily identifiable.

D *Bi-angular oblique perspective.* The flattening out is of the order of 45° (Breuil's 'semi-twisted perspective'). Common in Style III (Lascaux, Le Gabillou, Pech-Merle).

E *Uni-angular perspective.* This corresponds to the linear perspective of the classical arts: one single point of view situated a little in front of or behind the subject.

The respective positions of the four limbs are subject to a variety of formulas. If one draws them on a figure with the head to the left, the front legs numbered 1 and 2 and the rear 3 and 4, the first variation is $\frac{1\ 3}{2\ 4}$, which corresponds to the animal seen slightly from the front: it is the most common variation, attested in several hundred cases. The second formula $\frac{1\ 3}{2\ 4}$, corresponds to the animal seen slightly from behind. Though not the most frequent, this formula is to be found widely (Lascaux, Les Combarelles, Altamira, Ekaïn). The third and fourth variations, $\frac{1\ 3}{2\ 4}$ and

$\frac{1}{2}\frac{4}{3}$ are apparently accidental, for we find examples of each among figures in uni-angular perspective (Niaux, Salon Noir). Obviously only subjects with parallel limbs, essentially vertical, are considered so as not to confuse with subjects which might be expressing movement.

This classification, based on the reduction of angles of vision, broadly takes account of the evolution of palaeolithic art, with uni-angular perspective appearing later than the others and bi-angular oblique placed chronologically intermediate between bi-angular direct and uni-angular. This chronological sequence ought not to be applied without certain precautions: while it is hardly thinkable that one would find a bison in analytical figurative and uni-angular perspective in the Aurignacian, it is, on the other hand, theoretically possible that one might see bovines in the Magdalenian with horns corresponding to one of the earlier categories: children's drawings are there to induce caution. The perspective of horns or antlers is important, but it ought to be backed up by other criteria.

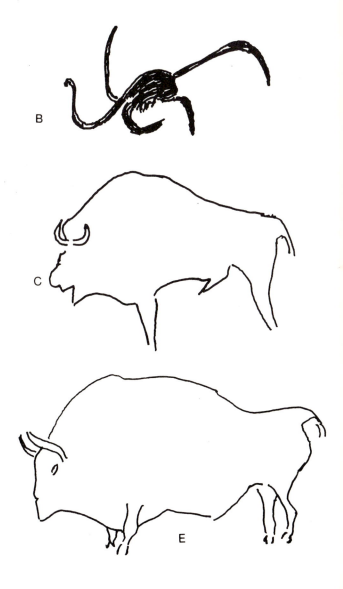

12. Perspective. A. Simple profile, Belcayre (Dordogne), Aurignacian.
B. Bi-angular opposed perspective, mammoth, La Baume Latrone (Gard).
C. Bi-angular direct perspective, bison, La Grèze (Dordogne).
D. Bi-angular oblique perspective, bison, La Mouthe (Dordogne).
E. Uni-angular perspective, bison, Font-de-Gaume (Dordogne).
(A, D and E inverted.)

The use of the traditional vocabulary of psychologists and art historians could not be adopted. For the distinguishing of figurative states, expressions like realism, schematism and naturalism, which are useful in the treatment of a general subject, only respond partially to the needs of an analysis as particular as that of primitive art. Luquet's 'intellectual realism' responds to a genuine reality; but why should it correspond to the form the furthest removed from the real? Why, moreover, should it be so inconvenient as to mix simple profile, multi-angular opposed perspective, bi-angular direct and bi-angular oblique perspective all in a single category, comparing primitive art as a whole with civilised art, when analysis should rather be based on a systematic plan stripped of value judgements?

THE HUMAN FIGURE AND PERSPECTIVE

Human figures are not common in cave art, a few dozen including the engravings on plaques of mobiliary type. A certain proportion of them consists of faces from front view or in profile. The body is rarely represented, apart from the female figures in profile (Les Combarelles, plaques from Lalinde, La Gare de Couze and Gönnersdorf) which have no head and feet and which tend towards the geometric figurative. The body is also represented in a few profiles of people who

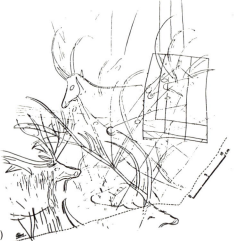

13. Lascaux, Apse. (Drawing by Glory.)

have been considered as masked 'sorcerers' (which could just as well be supernatural beings). The one from Les Trois-Frères has antlers on his head which are in bi-angular direct perspective in relation to a face drawn head-on, and are consequently in a perspective identifiable in relation to the rest of the body, which is in profile, as uni-angular perspective. The 'sorcerer' from Le Gabillou has a pair of bison horns on his head in bi-angular direct perspective, while the rest of the body, in profile, is in uni-angular perspective, though offering one of the variations in relationship between the four limbs of which two (the arms) are seen from the front, and the other two (the legs) from the back.

In contrast with the animal figures, the human figures do not conform to a well-defined stereotype (except for the enigmatic group of heads of two people in simple profile, one at least

34

apparently laughing, from the caves at Rouffignac, Font-de-Gaume, Fontanet and Les Combarelles). Analysis of the different images of man demonstrates a fact, certainly significant and which has, moreover, struck prehistorians for a long time: the plastic quality of the human figures is, as a whole, inferior to that of the animals. In addition, figures drawn face-on, or those facially dominant, stand at an inferior figurative level to figures in profile or predominantly in profile. This difference in level could be related to reasons of psycho-motory training. Indeed, the identification of animals at a distance is easier in profile than from the front. The outline, based on the cervico-dorsal curve, shaped the mental picture of the hunter, and the best of the human figures are those which have benefited from practice on animal figures like the Trois-Frères 'sorcerer'. The representation of the human head face-on is tied up with the representation of foreshortening, a difficulty in all periods. It is probably this difficulty which explains the relative rarity of front-facing human figures in palaeolithic art.

The same difficulty is found for animals. Face-on figures are actually very rare in parietal art

14. Lascaux, Apse, reindeer panel. (Drawing by Glory.)

35

(horse from Lascaux, small feline from Le Gabillou, a feline from Les Trois-Frères). This fact is all the more striking because in mobiliary art it is the face-on figures which in general are the source of themes of a geometric character.

The study of perspective in palaeolithic parietal art has turned out to be more complex than one might have supposed at the start. It is not always easy to unravel the different ways in which framing, partial superimposition and perpendiculars determine the first stages of perspective, but when one bears in mind the interest of palaeolithic artists in the expression of the third dimension, it should not seem too surprising that at a still precocious period, in the Upper Solutrean (before 15,000 BC), the problem of individual perspective should be among the major preoccupations of artists, nor that in the Middle and Late Magdalenian (from 13,000 to about 9000 BC) the optical solution of perspective should be resolved in forms which would not be seen again until several millennia later, at the dawn of the great civilisations.

GENERAL CONSIDERATIONS

The present study is directed towards research into the technical and aesthetic characteristics of the works, without consideration of their ideological content. Research into the meaning of paintings, engravings and sculptures on the walls of caves and rock shelters has been, and should remain, one of the principal objectives of the ethnology of the past – works of art being the only evidence which could enlighten us on certain fundamental aspects of the mental behaviour of Upper Palaeolithic man – but the other objective is the uncovering of facts concerning technical life. In fact, all that we know of technology, economy, social organisation, religion and aesthetic activities is based on the one hand on the use of the images, and on the other on the interpretation of those tools which have survived to our day. As a creator of symbols and as a creator of the means of manipulating material, either living or inert, Upper Palaeolithic man (our close ancestor) has been, for a century, the object of attempts at ethnographic reconstruction based primarily on his art. Rather paradoxically, the artistic techniques themselves have only almost incidentally been the objects of investigation. Their importance has been seen in their most concrete aspects (tools of execution, colouring materials) often only in a very superficial manner. The pictorial execution (thorough analysis of styles) has been rather neglected up to now, especially in those areas touching on concepts of space (framing, symmetry, perspective) and the expression of time (animation). Research in this direction should help to shed light on the substance of the message preserved on cave walls.

Assemblage (for space) and animation (for time), once disengaged from aspects associated with technique, seem to be very useful elements for measuring the degree of spatio-temporal symbolism in palaeolithic art. Research into the relationships between the technique and the object drawn, in other words the means used to adapt the image to the constraints of its support, and the quantitative analysis of the figures, all contribute to the definition of the substance of the message.

It is at first sight paradoxical that certain occurrences like superimposition seem to be the evidence of the existence of the message in showing that, in cases determined most often by the relative exiguity of the field available, superimposition was in some way enforced, sacrificing the legibility of the message. This technique, which results in the confusion of numerous figures,

perhaps explains their frequency on the small plaques which are by their nature exiguous
supports, and it seems to have played the same role in the Lascaux Nave or in the long corridor at Les Combarelles. Finally, it is clear that juxtaposition is the spontaneous reaction of the artist, but that he played around with different ways to arrive, if not at the legibility of the figures, at least at a preservation of the intelligibility of the message.

In a totally different direction, we have studied certain elements in order to try to recover the mental vision which palaeolithic man might have had of space as expressed in the drawings. One important and at first sight unusual fact is that the line of the ground-surface has not up till now been found painted or engraved, and yet in a number of cases a fissure or a ledge in the wall has indisputably been used to define the ground-surface. This occurrence might lead one to believe that perhaps the artist thought it natural to position his figures on the ground-surface suggested by existing fissures, but that the ideas of a ground-surface artificially expressed did not occur to him (probably for complex reasons).

At the end of this analysis of the idea of space there has been occasion to develop the concept of perspective. The moment of its appearance is difficult to fix, but apparently in the Upper Solutrean (Roc-de-Sers) or in the earliest Magdalenian (15,000–13,000 BC), the four limbs and the cranial appendages already obeyed fairly precise rules of perspective (Lascaux): the high point was around Magdalenian IV (12,000–10,000 BC). We are present at the acquisition of a perspective vision in which the four feet of the animal subject rest on the sole of the foot and no longer on the point, arranged in such a way that the polygon of sustentation is suggested.

Animation and time

The translation into images of the movement of isolated or grouped beings is the only process which can suggest the passing of time. In protohistoric and historic periods the spatio-temporal translation of an action leads from the mythogram to the pictogram and to a variety of forms of linear signs which are characteristic of writing. There is absolutely nothing to suggest that palaeolithic works could have been writing in the proper sense, but it has been unanimously accepted over the last three-quarters of a century that palaeolithic artists wanted to express something and not just to scribble on the walls of their cave. It is not essential to specify the significance of what they transformed into graphic symbols (animals, people or signs). The assemblages of figures can belong to a *mythogram*, without absolute spatio-temporal references, and to a *pictogram*, an isolated figure or a group of figures expressing an action synthesising 'a before, a during and an after', like the wounded bison with bent knees at Niaux, or the famous 'scene in the shaft' at Lascaux. The following stage would be the *pictographic chain*, expressed by a series of pictograms forming a sequence like a strip-cartoon, and the *ideogram*, which already belongs to writing in the strict sense of a sign capable of being rendered in a linear way, whose content is a second degree abstraction (like the image of a horse, the first degree of abstraction, which is extended to the second degree, as a symbol of speed).

Animation is not a rarity in palaeolithic art, but it occurs in isolated instances, even if there are several animated figures in a single group. The great ceiling at Altamira contains about twenty bisons in various postures without it being possible to establish a collective activity. Save for a few rare exceptions which we shall examine, there are no scenes in the Palaeolithic other than that in 93 the Shaft at Lascaux where a bison is drawn disembowelled by a spear blow while tossing a man. The links between this tragic scene and the figure of a rhinoceros which occupies the left of the panel are not clear, and it is likely that this rhinoceros is irrelevant to the hunter's misadventure. This actual scene probably constituted an important and durable mythological theme, since we know of four pictographic versions spread through the Charente and the Dordogne. Chronologically the sculpted frieze of Le Roc-de-Sers would be the earliest example as it is Upper Solutrean (about 17,000 BC); Villars and Lascaux with their Style III figures follow; for Lascaux, radiocarbon dating has allowed the period of activity to be fixed at 15,000 BC. It would seem plausible to presume about five centuries of occupation of the cave, which must have been closed up quite rapidly, after the beginning of the Magdalenian. The fourth example of the scene of the charging bison is an object of reindeer antler on which is engraved a scene where we can see a bison struck by a spear blow and a man lying on the ground behind the animal. From the stylistic point of view it seems that here we have a more recent object (Style IV) of around 12,000 BC.

The possession of four versions of the theme of man and bison allows a few interesting observations on temporal integration in decorated space. Perhaps the most interesting is that the temporal sequence suggested is not fixed in a rigid manner by a strictly iconographic tradition. Moreover, one can discern the expression of an oral tradition which allows the artist the freedom of the descriptive episode. The rarity of 'scenes' in mobiliary art as well as in cave art makes it necessary to observe figures individually in order to determine the part played by animation in the whole of parietal art.

Conventionally all details allowing the reconstruction of a spatio-temporal sequence with regard to one figure have been taken as proof of animation. Such is the case, for example, for a fallen animal, which according to its attitude is dead, giving rise to the whole spatio-temporal sequence which separates it from the point and instant when it was still alive. I think the definition can be extended, though retaining the distinction, to the animals bearing wounds but no other indication of animation.

A relatively simple framework allows a description of the quality of the figures related to the realism of the behaviour: *nil animation, symmetrical animation, segmentary animation* and *coordinated animation*. This terminology is enough to demonstrate, from the beginning to the end of palaeolithic art, a very tangible evolution of the processes of animation and of the number of animated individuals.

Nil animation

Rather paradoxically, it is nil animation that seems to offer the most difficulties of taxonomic subdivision. A first distinction can be made between subjects in *vertical rigid extension*, the usual case for figures of Styles I and II with extremities pointing towards the ground or not drawn, and later subjects whose attitude corresponds to natural immobility, *vertical posed extension*. A large number of Style III figures have perpendiculars not actually vertical but more, or less, oblique for the front legs than for the back (firmly planted position). The great Lascaux bulls and the spotted Pech-Merle horses are good examples of *oblique rigid extension*.

Symmetrical animation

Symmetrical animation through the extension of the four limbs ('flying gallop') can be seen in a few rare examples (boar from Altamira, ibex, goat and kid on the Rouffignac ceiling). It is not impossible that the horses in the left-hand part of the Hall of the Bulls at Lascaux, with front legs raised but back legs upright might have been meant by the painters to be galloping, but it is more likely that, as for the second 'Chinese horse' in the Axial Passage, the raising of the forelegs represents one of the phases of the nuptial display. Symmetrical animation through the bending of all four legs corresponds to drawings of animals lying down or collapsed, feet bent back, in an attitude of rest or agony. Examples in parietal art are not common (Chabot, Teyjat, Niaux) but there are evidently more in mobiliary art, in particular of engraving on objects where it is necessary to fit into a volume or surface which is technically defined. This fact corroborates the

82

15. 80

81

42

84. 92

hypothesis, already formulated, that in the majority of cases the animated image is determined by the scope of the frame rather than by a 'canon' of strictly traditional character. Confirmation of this can already be seen in mobiliary art, for example the spear-throwers from Bedeilhac and Enlène, showing an ibex with feet bent back, and the spear-thrower from Arudy, an ibex with extended feet. In parietal art, the example of the three 'bounding' bisons at Altamira (in reality bisons rolling in the dust) show the application of the same principle: three bosses on the ceiling of suitable shape inspired the creation of these exceptional figures.

Segmentary animation

93 Much more curious is animation restricted to the significant part of the body. The example of the bison in the Lascaux shaft is perhaps the most extraordinary. From its general outline it is an animal of the type with four limbs in rigid extension, with the body in uni-angular perspective,

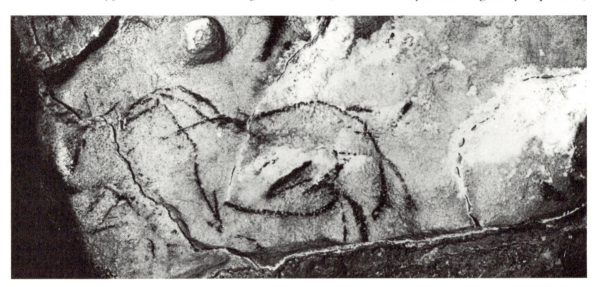

15. Altamira. Horse in Style III, no. 53.

seen slightly from behind, and the extremities in bi-angular direct perspective. The horns are in bi-angular oblique perspective, as is the rule for horns at Lascaux. Movement is strictly limited to the tail, which thrashes the air, and to the head, which has undergone a rotation of 90° bringing the beard against the forehead.

Most frequently it is the limbs which are the subject of segmentary animation. An example is the horse at the end of Gallery 3 at Le Portel with its left foreleg raised at a right angle, another is the aurochs engraved on a schist plaque from Chaleux (Belgium). Segmentary animation of the two forelegs can also be seen at Lascaux: horse 577 in the Apse and horse 24 on the panel of the Black Cow in the Nave trot with great strides of the front legs while the rest of the body, and
87, 88 particularly the back legs, remains immobile. No less interesting is horse 110 in hollow E in the Passage, where the forelegs give a plausible impression of trotting while the right hind leg is bent, not at the hock but in the centre of the cannon-bone, which is bent round like a hairpin.

The head and shoulders constitute an important element in animation, all the more because the carriage of the head can be different according to the species (horizontal shoulders of reindeer,

40

raised shoulders of stag, etc.). The carriage of the head clearly shows the sequence of actions which will take place in the immediate future: the attitude of listening which precedes a charge or a flight; the lowered head of a carnivore following a trail; the reindeer from Thayngen (on a pierced bâton) and the horse from Angles-sur-l'Anglin who follow the scent of a female with their noses to the ground. There are several examples of animals with their heads turned back (hind from the Abri Murat, stag from Lortet, fawn from Bedeilhac, bison from La Madeleine), though all these are mobiliary pieces, and animals like this are more rare in parietal art. A good example is the lying-down bison of Altamira. For this and the preceding examples the reason for the innovation seems to have been the necessity of resolving a problem of framing (through a lack of space or technical constraints). For the most part the animals are immobile, but encountering

16. Laugerie-Basse, plaque. Male reindeer following a female.

some element in the support seems to have provoked the artist's imagination. Thus the only example of a mammoth holding its trunk horizontally (Arcy-sur-Cure) is determined by the shapes on the wall suggesting on the one hand an ear clearly standing out from the support and, on the other, the evocation of a trunk: the engraver only had to complete it, by adding an eye, a few hairs under the trunk and the beginning of the tusks. On the theme of segmentary animation one can compare feline 51 from Les Combarelles, with immobile features, and the felines from Le Gabillou and Labastide, with their yawning mouths and bared fangs.

Certain painted or engraved figures have parallel or diverging lines in front of their snout or muzzle, which prehistorians have, with some justification, taken for the breath of the animal. This sign is as well attested in mobiliary art (horse on the Laugerie-Basse spatula, ibex on the Isturitz spatula) as it is in parietal art (bisons from Bernifal and Peña de Los Hornos, aurochs from Pech-Merle, feline 57 from the Passage of the Felines at Lascaux). Mention must also be made of the two

125

bears at Les-Trois Frères, crippled with wounds and vomiting blood. Finally, to complete the list of bodily emissions, there is feline 57, which marks its territory by emitting a jet of urine.

The body is not subjected to segmentary animation, for its contours are not suitable for major bending movements, but to a certain extent it is possible to include in drawing of a temporal nature the presence of wounds, which will be the subject of examination later.

As a final detail on segmentary animation comes the tail, which, for most species, transmits the degree of the animal's excitement. The bison provides the largest number of examples, with all possible positions represented. A curious fact is that there are only very few cases of horses with moving tails. The most odd is one of the 'ponies' from the Axial Passage at Lascaux, whose tail, raised to the horizontal, is inserted between the ears of the horse which follows and the back right hoof of the 'leaping' cow. Once more, the innovation has come about through not wishing to encroach on neighbouring figures. Some more cases, among others, are the mammoth (Pech-Merle), the rhinoceros (Lascaux), the ibex (Cougnac, Rouffignac) and cervids (reindeer from Las Monedas, hind from Levanzo).

Coordinated animation

Figures in which themes of segmentary animation are linked to portray the complete behaviour of the animal are relatively rare. Attempts at coordination are mainly concerned with the movement of feet, corresponding to *lateral coordinated animation* and *diagonal coordinated animation*,
16 according to which the limbs are positioned in twos on the same side (left front, left back) or
17 alternately (left front, right back). Both formulas are found, particularly in Style IV (Middle and Late Magdalenian), but the elements are not always sufficient to be certain that it is not by chance. What is not in doubt is the ever increasing preoccupation with representing movement during the course of the evolution of Upper Palaeolithic art. This tendency is even more obvious with *complex coordinated animation* in which head and tail can be involved as well as the limbs. At the beginning of Style IV, in the scene in the Shaft at Lascaux, the bison offers an example of ultra-segmentary animation in which only the head and tail transmit movement, while in the Late Magdalenian, at Limeuil or Thayngen, the reindeer sniffing the ground is integrated in a movement which animates all parts of the body.

17. Teyjat. Cow and bull.

The Message

Consideration of technique, form, space and time has enabled the investigation of one side of palaeolithic parietal art. We think that data have emerged from it which far exceed the simple examination of techniques. The complexity of the links between the figures, the games with superimposition and oblique perspective have led us to assume the existence of an organisation for the assemblages of figures which makes of them ideologically pertinent entities. Once Palaeolithic man is adjudged to have woven a web of relationships between elements in the parietal ensembles, then the palaeolithic specialist has the authority to seek out the nature and significance of these relationships.

Parietal cave art has an exceptional peculiarity, which is that the works have remained in the place where the artist created them in often good and occasionally miraculous conditions of preservation. The figures that were engraved, sculpted or painted must have signified something, even if they seem to have been produced without any apparent order. Simply looking at several of the parietal assemblages leaves one with the impression that the significance of the groups of figures would clearly emerge in response to the right questions. If these reflections are valid for the animal figures then they should be even more so for the signs that we find in nearly all the decorated caves in a more or less developed form and in variable numbers. The 'assemblies' of signs, like those at Lascaux, Cougnac, El Castillo and La Pasiega, imply an absolutely indisputable intention on the part of those who created them to produce something significant.

Made up of animal figures and signs distributed in subterranean space (and in rock shelters where they have rarely survived) the parietal assemblages have the essential characteristics of a message; they respond to the needs and means that man has had since the Upper Palaeolithic to produce oral symbols in a material form by using his hands.

Since 1958, the date when the first outline of 'the function of signs in palaeolithic sanctuaries' appeared, I have pursued research into the form, if not the meaning, of the palaeolithic message. The second stage was the publication of *Préhistoire de l'art occidental*, which in 1965 marked an 'intermediate' stage in the theory, preceded in 1964 by *Les religions de la préhistoire* and followed in 1966 by *Reflexions de méthode sur l'art paléolithique*. In 1968, at the International Symposium on

Rupestral Art in Barcelona, I published a discussion on *Les signes pariétaux du Paléolithique supérieur franco-cantabrique*, in particular on the probable existence of a third category of signs, essentially dots (S^3), a detail which has since been confirmed. Finally, in 1972, at the Symposium in Santander my *Considérations sur l'organisation spatiale des figures animales dans l'art pariétal paléolithique* recorded research into a theoretical picture of the links between the different parts of the assemblages. Since this last publication I have been concentrating on the problems of space and time which are to be found in the first part of this book. In the following pages I shall undertake research into a model for figurative construction which can at the same time demonstrate the unity of the groupings in palaeolithic parietal decoration and also bring out what is particular to different periods and regions. For this the following plan is proposed:

The actors: animals, humans, monsters; the signs; the assemblages.

The Actors

ANIMALS

The list of animal species is presented here not in the zoological order but according to their numerical frequency, for it is less useful to know that the reindeer is a cervid than to know that it occupies eighth position in the total of animal figures. This listing, in comparison with the animals most represented in the form of bone remains on the majority of settlement sites, raises questions of the representative nature of lists of animals in art. At the start one can examine a possible parallel with the traditions of the whole of Europe, where the lion and the eagle, rare and mediocre forms of food, are nevertheless much more commonly represented in western heraldic art than the calf or the pig. We shall return to this question, but there are good reasons to suppose that the drawings of palaeolithic animals constituted a bestiary rather than a collection of edible species.

It would be illusory to hope to give an absolute number of the figures at different sites for many reasons, such as the inevitable destruction of part of the works and the frequent difficulties of identification. But it has been established with certainty that, to within a few per cent, the relationships between the different species make up three numerically decreasing groups: 1. equids and bovines, 2. cervids, caprids and mammoth, 3. felines, ursines and rhinoceros.

Group A. Uniquely comprises equids, and in practice the horse. Attempts to distinguish
90 morphological types have only a very hypothetical basis. Variations from one image to another
92 are such that they defy almost all zoological interpretation. On the other hand, two equids with long ears, one at Lascaux and the other at Les Trois-Frères, do not rule out the representation of an ass-type or a hemione. By itself the horse represents nearly 30% of parietal animals. Throughout human history equids have been, if not the most abundant game, at least the most constant. Their presence in practically *all* parietal assemblages, and their numerical preponderance are a gauge of the importance they had in the figurative hierarchy. Their primary sexual characteristics are only rarely, if ever, figured, but we have seen under 'symmetrical animation' that the representation of the preliminary manifestations of mating implied the presence of males and females possibly in couples.

Group B. Comprising bovines (bison and aurochs or wild ox), this second group also represents

45

about 30% of the figures. The bison (23% of all figures) accounts for nearly 80% of the total number of bovines (aurochs 16.2% of bovines). Representation of the two bovines is not the same in all the caves. Some have the aurochs as the principal bovine with one or several bisons (Lascaux), but the majority of assemblages is dedicated to the bison with the possible intervention of aurochs (Niaux). This 'general post' of the two large ruminants is difficult to explain, but it is certain that at Lascaux the bison only occurs in the deeper areas (Axial Passage, Apse, Shaft, Nave, Passage of the Felines) while at Niaux the aurochs is only represented by two engravings on clay, in areas far removed from the assemblages of bisons, and one painted head in the Cartailhac Gallery, itself also isolated.

91, 94   The *bison*, in a relatively large number of cases, is represented in unusual positions; vertically, it totals by itself nearly 50% of the 67 unusual positions established, while only 6 horses out of a total horse population of more than 600 figure in this way.

89   The aurochs (B²) is far less common (less than 150) than the bison (more than 500). It is not apparently more common in Cantabria and Asturia than in the Pyrenees and Aquitaine, but it predominates in the centre and south of Spain. It also predominates in the Ardèche and in Italy. It is present in Périgord, in great numbers at Lascaux (87 aurochs as against 20 bison) and rather discreetly at Les Combarelles (2 examples); at Font-de-Gaume 8 aurochs and about 50 bisons make up the bovine population, while at Fourneau-de-Diable there are three examples between the Solutrean and Final Magdalenian (Limeuil, plaque).

Group C. Horses and bisons can be counted in hundreds, but the animals of group C are much less than this in total: the *stag* (C¹ᵃ) and the *hind* (C¹ᵇ) are respectively 5.1% and 6.2% of all figures.

98   There are stag–hind pairs in several Spanish caves (deep gallery at Altamira, La Pasiega A). One
117   also finds male and female couples of *megaceros* (deer with giant antlers) at Cougnac and Pech-Merle; but often stag and hind seem to play their role separately (as in fact they do much of the time in real life). This is the case at Lascaux, where hinds and stags occupy topographically different areas, and at Las Chimeneas, where the single painted hind is to be found under a fold in the wall of the main room while 5 stags are concentrated in a passage some distance away. This peculiarity of separation is found again in the archaic period at Covalanas, where 17 hinds constitute the main element of the bestiary, accompanying an aurochs, a horse, and a figure difficult to identify. In the latest period (Late Magdalenian) at Teyjat several stags are grouped on engraved plaques 1 and 2. It should be noted that the stag is clearly more common than the reindeer.

96   The *mammoth* (C²) (9.3%) is represented unevenly but consistently in all areas except central and southern Spain and Italy. It can amount to more than 100 individuals in Périgord (Rouffignac) or be limited to a single example as at Domme, El Castillo or Pindal. In these last two caves the single proboscidian, situated in the deepest part of the cave, gives the impression of a planned isolation. A few sites have mammoths as the most common animal numerically: Arcy-sur-Cure, Bernifal, Pech-Merle and Chabot. This point will be taken up again later.

31, 64   The *ibex* (C³) (8.4%), like other group C animals, is a 'complementary' animal whose role is
109   apparently to complete the assemblages of the significant elements of groups A and B. It is often found in a lateral position in relation to the bison. The best example of this lateral relationship is at Niaux where, in each of the large painted panels, there are one or two ibexes alongside or framing a bison.

18. Table of the principal characteristics of Style IV.

A. North. Arcy-sur-Cure. B. Poitou-Périgord. 1. Les Combarelles, Angles-sur-l'Anglin, Cap Blanc, Lascaux (Shaft). 2. Les Combarelles, Rouffignac. 3. Teyjat. C. Pyrenees. 1. Massoulas, Niaux, Labastide. 2. Les Trois-Frères, Le Portel. D. Spain. 1. Altamira, Santimamine. 2. Las Chimeneas, El Pindal, Los Casares.

The *reindeer* (C⁴) is only represented by 3.8% of all figures, which is rather paradoxical for this animal which has given its name to the Upper Palaeolithic – the 'Age of the Reindeer'. The Abbé Breuil had already noticed at Niaux the contrast between the abundance of cervid bones in the Magdalenian settlements in the region and the total absence of reindeer among the figures decorating the cave. The same experience was repeated at Lascaux, where numerous bones, the debris of eating, were found on the Magdalenian floor-level (which was contemporary with the paintings and engravings) and these were almost exclusively of reindeer, while the walls could only produce a single and dubious image of this animal. At Rouffignac, the last figure in the cave, a good kilometre from the entrance, is a reindeer drawn with the finger on the soft wall. A single reindeer is also the final figure in the Le Portel cave. In contrast the reindeer is present, if not abundant at Font-de-Gaume and at Les Combarelles which is contemporary, at Les Trois-Frères which is close to Le Portel in time and space, and in Spain even as far as Asturia (Tito Bustillo).

Group D. A new level in the frequency of animal figures appears with species which can scarcely be counted in tens. These are the bear, the feline and the rhinoceros, which the Abbé Breuil had noticed were preferentially placed in remote areas.

The *bear* (D) (1.6%) is often considered to be a representation of a cave bear, but it is probably not, for this apparently peaceable omnivore had already, if not disappeared, at least been threatened with extinction at the beginning of the Magdalenian. Of the millions of long scratch-marks which it left on the walls in the depths of the caves where it hibernated, none cut through works of art which might have been there. On the other hand we know of engravings which cut into scratch-marks (Aldène). The bear pictured by the Magdalenians was in all probability *Ursus arctos*, which is still living. Its position in subterranean space is rather inconsistent. At Les Combarelles it appears in little groups in the bends in the gallery, but not in the deepest part. At Le Gabillou, it is a little before the end, at the point where the reindeer appear. At Venta de la Perra, the bear is engraved a few metres from the entrance, at Lascaux a small black bear is concealed in the ventral line of the third large bull in the first room.

The *feline* (D²) (1.3%) numbers some 30 examples spread through all regions except Italy. It is nowhere numerous. Lascaux has 6 (or 7) and Les Trois-Frères at least 4. At Les Combarelles there is one in each of the last assemblages in the second and third galleries. All the feline figures known are situated in distant positions, either in a separate room (Les Trois-Frères) or in a deep passage (Font-de-Gaume, Lascaux), or on the outer edge of an assemblage (Labastide). At Le Gabillou, the two felines are in the first part of the cave, but as at Les Combarelles, at the end of an assemblage which coincides with the end of a first sequence in the cave.

The *rhinoceros* (D³) (0.7%). About twenty examples, amongst which Rouffignac accounts for more than half. It is therefore a rare animal. Disregarding the painted or engraved rhinoceroses of Rouffignac, one comes across only isolated examples like those at Les Combarelles (near feline 51), at Font-de-Gaume (at the back, not far from the feline), at Lascaux (at the bottom of the Shaft), at Los Casares (on the edge of an assemblage of animals with the main one an aurochs) and at Les Trois-Frères (on the edge of a panel of bisons and horses).

Other animal subjects fall to a proportion of less than 0.5%. These are *monsters* (E) (0.4%), *birds* (O) (0.2%) and *fish* (P) (0.3%). *Monsters* are either anthropomorphic figures, with an animal head, like the 'sorcerer' of Les Trois Frères or that at Le Gabillou, or, at Pergouset, the character with a man's body but the neck and head replaced by a sort of tube or tail, which evokes, on the one hand another monster from the same cave reduced to a tail lifted up above an anus furnished with long hairs, and, on the other, the 'women-bisons' from Pech-Merle. Pergouset is an extreme case, for there one also sees an amoeba-like creature with a vaguely human outline, a hind with an exceptionally long neck, and a rather equine animal head mounted on a giraffe neck. This theme of the animal with immoderately long neck is also found at Labastide, Altxerri and Le Gabillou. It also appears at Le Gabillou in the guise of a quadruped with a body and head which defies identification. Neither is it reasonable to try to identify the Lascaux 'unicorn' or the Pech-Merle 'antelopes'.

Fish are exceedingly rare in cave art: the species represented are salmon types (Le Portel, Niaux), pike (Pech-Merle), sole or dab (Mas-d'Azil) and indeterminate fish (Altxerri). The Pindal fish is more of a monster, for it is salmon-like but the fins are elongated into sickle shapes like those of a tuna.

Birds are rare. Night hunters are represented by the owls of Les Trois-Frères and the one at Le Portel. In the lower cave at Isturitz there is the head and neck of a crow, painted black and with the beak part-open.

Reptiles, which are present in mobiliary art, are apparently missing in parietal art, unless one considers as serpents the few round heads which finish off some of the meanders drawn with a finger on one of the Rouffignac ceilings. Nor are there are known amphibians.

As a whole, parietal art has a slightly less extensive register than mobiliary art where one finds the *chamois*, many *fish* (nearly all salmon), *snakes*, a *frog* and even a *grasshopper* (Les Trois-Frères). Some animals whose existence is proved by bone remains were either never drawn or were very limited in number. Among the cervids the *megaceros*, a deer with giant antlers, is an example, for it is only figured in three cases (Cougnac, Pech-Merle, Pair-non-Pair(?)). The *elk* is only known from one unconfirmed drawing (Pergouset), the *chamois* is apparently missing, the other antelope, the *saiga* is only represented by one head (Les Combarelles II). The *boar* is only represented by the famous one on the ceiling at Altamira (and this is contested because it has bison horns). Among the carnivores (other than the *felines*) the *wolf*, whose bones are found everywhere on settlement sites, is completely missing apart from two exceptions (Font-de-Gaume, Les Combarelles 114). A *fox* is featured at Altxerri and a *musteline* of the marten or ferret type was discovered in the new gallery (Clastres gallery) at Niaux. The *hyena* is totally absent. This could be due to the fact that the hyena had probably already disappeared by the time of the development of subterranean art. Whatever the reasons for the abundance or absence of those animals figured in relation to their real presence or abundance, a certain logic appears in the simple examination of the lists. The absolutely consistent presence of the horse and the no less consistent presence of one of the two bovines, bisons or aurochs, even of both, is corroborated by the fact that each of the two series represents roughly a third of the elements in the whole bestiary (A–horse 27%, B–bison + aurochs 28%, making 55%). The third group (C–stag and hind 11% + mammoth 9.3%, ibex 8.4%, reindeer 3.8%, making 32.5%) defines a level far below the first and the second, but its total is also equivalent to just about a third of the whole. The fourth group (D–bear 1.6%, feline 1.3%, rhinoceros 0.7%, making 3.6%) accentuates an even more obvious drop. As for the groups of monsters (M–0.4%), fish (P–0.3%) and bird (0–0.2%), their qualification in the bestiary is somewhat furtive. This quantitative presentation of the animals must be thought of as a first empirical model. It represents, in fact, the whole inventory of the species present in France, Spain and Italy. The form taken by this amalgam suggests a variety of hypotheses. Is the presence of the complete list (A–B–C–D) at each site demonstrable, or is only a part of the grouping found in the quantitative order of the list? In other words, is the combination A–B–C–D quantitatively valid or can one find the combination D–C–B–A or, quite otherwise, C–A, A–C etc.?

If we consider the near-70 decorated caves which are sufficiently well preserved to allow acceptance that the different animal species could be significant, we can make a certain number of observations. The horse is present everywhere (69/69). Bovines are distributed in a less absolute manner, but the large ruminants are represented at all the sites (69/69), whether by one (bison alone 32/69), by the other (aurochs alone 17/69) or by both. This is what leads us to see in these three animals (horse, bison, aurochs) the fundamental formula of the palaeolithic bestiary. The absence of the horse (cave of La Vache at Bidon) and of the large ruminant (La Baume Latrone, Gard, and the cave of La Forêt at Tursac, Dordogne) are exceptions which bring out even more clearly the remarkable uniformity of the A–B formula. The cave at Le Cougnac, basically made up of mammoths, cervids (megaceros, stag and ibex) probably involves, like the previous examples, a problem of preservation, but this easy argument may not be the explanation. For the same reasons the existence of 'heretical' combinations, if it cannot be rejected, cannot arbitrarily fill this gap in the bestiary.

The stag and the hind are represented 21 and 16 times respectively. Nine sites have both animals, separated or in pairs. The other cases relate to caves where only one of the animals is represented. At Lascaux, for example, the 85 stags occupy different situations from those of the 3 hinds counted. The stag and the hind are relatively more frequent in Spain, which could be explained on climatic grounds. but as many are found in Périgord (sites like Lascaux, Les Combarelles and Teyjat) as in Quercy (sites like Pech-Merle and Cougnac), and in the Pyrenees (sites like Niaux and Les Trois-Frères). Even in the assemblages of 'cold' animals like reindeer, mammoth and woolly rhinoceros, the stag is present.

The ibex occurs at 37 sites, 26 times accompanied by bison and 25 times by aurochs or both. The ibex figures frequently on the same list of caves as the stag; it is missing at Teyjat, and not common in the group of caves with tectiform signs, that is, Font-de-Gaume, Bernifal and Rouffignac. At this last site it is confined to the border of the painted ceiling, and at Les Combarelles to groups 20 and 45.

MAN AND WOMAN

99, 100 101 Human representations were called 'anthropomorphs' by prehistorians, at a time when their degree of human dignity could still have been disputed. The number of useful occurrences is about 75 in parietal art and just about the same in mobiliary art. The figurative states of this population reveal a fact which has struck prehistorians: that is the poor plastic quality of the works. The *pure geometric* is represented first of all by the geometric signs which will be the subject of the next chapter. Some of the small statuettes from Mezin in the Ukraine, which are very simply modelled, have a pubic triangle which is integrated into a purely geometric decorative scheme. The pure geometric is unidentifiable without a context, and one frequently concludes that the character key to the identification is a degree ahead of the rest of the drawing. This is the case for the cranial appendages of some animals (horns or antlers) which ensure the means of identifying

50

the subject. The example of the Mezin statuettes is no different, and the character-key can be seen a degree ahead or behind the general figurative state of the figurine.

The *geometric figurative* is well illustrated by the man overturned by the bison in the Shaft at Lascaux. The figure is entirely constructed of straight lines roughly joined together to result in a 'matchstick' man. The detail of the sex has very probably been included simply as a detail of identification. This figure contrasts strongly with the rhinoceros and the bison which frame it, which are in analytical figurative.

The *synthetic figurative* is the state which describes many of the human figures, whether parietal or mobiliary. The curves have a complete and simplifying modulation which often makes the sex identification difficult, particularly when it is applied to a single head or to a ghostly outline.

The *analytical figurative* corresponds to an adjusting of lines close to optical reality. It is almost non-existent for human figures, particularly for those on walls, although it exists in Magdalenian animal art. The proportion of analytical figurative to synthetic figurative suggests some subtle transitions. The passage from one state to the other is fairly well illustrated by the bas-relief or fully sculpted female figures known as 'Venus' figures, all characterised by a synthetic execution, particularly for the head and legs, but with a certain sort of analysis controlling the development of the synthetic forms.

The attributes of the human figure. Because they are uncommon in cave art and also infrequent in mobiliary art, the figures of humans have not yielded much information on their role in the palaeolithic message. The magic of the hunt, symbols of human fertility side by side on the walls with those of animals, a shaman executing hunting dances, mother goddesses, all these explanatory themes abound, and are based solely on the reminiscences of western thought. It seemed simpler and more prudent to seek out a mode of analysis which allows significant questions on the grouping of figures on the wall and on stone blocks or mobiliary plaques to arise. The following points have been taken into consideration.

Maxillary projection. Alongside figures with a circular or oval face we can see the development of a strongly marked prognathism which brings the bridge of the nose to the horizontal like the profile of a baboon. This sort of deformation is found in mobiliary art as well as in parietal. There are examples in the caves at Les Combarelles, the Angles-sur-l'Anglin shelter, the Commarque cave, on plaquettes from La Marche and from the Morin shelter, on an engraved pebble from La Madeleine and the sculpted heads from Kostienki. These figures have been seen as masked people. We can reject this hypothesis, however, since all stages between the normal face (Saint Cirq) and the completely animalised profile (Massat) have been documented. It could well be that we are seeing a tendency to idealise the human profile; and even if they are supernatural creatures, which can in no way be ruled out, there is no need to see them as masked.

19 *Cephalic appendages and various attributes.* The 'sorcerer' from the Les Trois-Frères cave whose body, which has human limbs, possesses the face of an owl, the tail of a horse and the antlers of a reindeer, has contributed by its strangeness to the generalised image of the sorcerer rigged up in animal skins. On the other hand, it would seem that the horned being constitutes a very rare

51

theme (apart from two other small engravings which are part of the same group of figures) and is to be seen only at Le Gabillou (with the head and tail of a bison) and on a plaque from Lourdes (with deer antlers and a fluttering tail).

Figures holding objects. The absence of objects in the hands of anthropomorphs is quite striking. One

19. Les Trois-Frères. Sorcerer. (Drawing by Breuil.)

can cite as exceptions the women in bas-relief at Laussel, one of whom is holding a bison horn and the other an unidentified curved object. An engraved bone plaque from Laugerie-Basse seems to show a person with disproportionate arms apparently siezing a salmon by the tail, an operation which in real life is rather hazardous. In contrast, the man carrying an elongated object on his shoulder (a stick or a spear) can be found among the Roc-de-Sers sculptures and on several mobiliary objects.

Bent bodies. An important number of masculine, feminine and neuter figures have the body bent forwards to around 30°–45°, particularly the somewhat abbreviated female figures of La Roche at Lalinde or the Gare de Couze, and the male or neuter figures like the animalised person no.81 at Les Combarelles or the Trois-Frères 'sorcerer'. The figures stuck with spears at Cougnac are also bent, but the one in the same state at Pech-Merle has an upright body.

102. 103

20. Les Trois-Frères. Section of the panel with the person with the musical bow. (Drawing by Breuil.)

One may also wonder about the reason why on many occasions figures have *bent legs*. In the case of the man fleeing in front of a bison at Roc-de-Sers the bending of the legs could signify the movement of flight, but it may also perhaps be an accident of framing, the available height of the field not allowing the straightening of the legs. The same goes for the 'sorcerer' at Le Gabillou and the man at Saint-Cirq.

Sex of the figures. Basing the identification of sex on primary or secondary (beard, for example) characteristics, definitely male figures represent 32%, female 18% and 'neuters' 50%. The attributes particular to certain figures permit at least a possible sex identification, but no less than one out of two figures show no defined sexual characteristics.

Obvious sex. This category comprises all the people that have primary sexual attributes. They only represent about a third of all anthropomorphic figures. Masculine figures are in roughly equivalent proportions in mobiliary and parietal art. Half of the sexed male figures are ithyphallic, which reduces this typological category to a few individuals (three for parietal art: Lascaux, the man in the Shaft, and Le Portel, two small people with their sex rendered by stalagmites). The representing of the penis erect does not seem really to be a predominant trait of male figures but rather one of the optional features which characterises the male figure in the assemblage.

Tail. The presence of a caudal appendage can be combined with other animal characteristics. The tail can also appear as the only animal feature, as at Hornos de la Peña. The idea of the tail is replaced in Quercy, at Pech-Merle, with a very peculiar variant: several figures grouped in a niche ending in a deep hole appear either as schematic bisons with raised tails or as females in profile with the head formed by the bison tail, depending on the direction from which you look at them. These women-bisons, repeated half a dozen times, could be viewed as an artist's joke were it not for the existence of an even stranger case in the Pergouset cave, a few kilometres from Pech-Merle. A masculine figure with visible sex was engraved on the wall, the stump of a tail planted between his shoulders in the guise of a head.

Vanquished man. Knocked over by bear or bison, pierced by the spears of human adversaries, the theme of vanquished man constitutes the most pictographic assemblage in palaeolithic art. It is clear that each of the three aggression themes could have had a different mythographic content. The fact that the pictographic theme is practically unique and occurs in two forms in parietal art (bison charging man at Lascaux and Villars, man transfixed at Pech-Merle and Cougnac), poses serious problems that we are not yet capable of resolving except through hypotheses which have little foundation.

Monsters.

The category of figures which perhaps most clearly marks the 'metaphysical' side of parietal imagery is that of the monsters. They are rare, but they indisputably exist. A number of them that have the human body as a base are found in mobiliary as well as in parietal art. One finds among them people with animal appendages (antlers or horns), with animal heads (bison at Le Gabillou, reindeer on the pebble from La Madeleine), with a face like a snout (Les Combarelles 81, Commarque); and whether they are masked or imaginary matters little for the present, for a masked person has an evocative power at least as great as that of the monster that he represents. We have seen above that these subjects are relatively rare. The most extraordinary human monster is the one at Pergouset with a human body, male, with his head replaced by a tube emerging from the shoulders. The wall in the area of this figure is covered with monstrous engravings: an amoeba-like figure, perhaps with a distant affinity with the drawing of the headless man, and superimposed a figure vaguely cephalomorphic but which represents an upright tail above an anus surrounded by hair. There is also a creature drawn with a long neck, topped with a head quite like a horse's head. This creature with a long neck but with a more simple head can also be found at Altxerri and Le Gabillou, and perhaps at Labastide where it is set on a huge body with an ill-defined outline. One could perhaps include in this idea of a long neck the 'antelopes' from Le Combel at Pech-Merle, three animals swollen like skin bottles with tiny caprid (?) heads. The famous Lascaux 'unicorn' with its prostrated spotted body, short-muzzled head and equally short tail, has for forty years defied the wisdom of the naturalists.

105

Except perhaps for the theme of the long neck, monsters do not seem to have been a common produce of palaeolithic artists. They do, however, shed some light on the imaginary in their

21. Lascaux, Apse. Male and female symbols.

period. If it were necessary to defend the attitude of artists towards symbolic thought, and to prove that they possessed oral traditions of the fantastic, then the monsters would be suitable for providing useful evidence.

THE SIGNS

The most impressive manifestation on the intellectual level is the presence in the great majority of palaeolithic art sites of painted or engraved geometric figures. The geometricism and the frequent graphic complexity of these signs contrasts with the drawing of the animal figures which exhibit the characteristics of an often very close analysis of living form. What these signs meant has not greatly concerned prehistorians. As their imagination has led them they have interpreted them as huts, traps, armour, boomerangs or harpoons, without taking note of the typological categories into which they divide: broad signs (S2), narrow signs (S1), dots (S3), and in particular of the existence of a model common to most – narrow signs of elongated form with or without lateral extensions (barbs, branches, hooks), and broad oval, triangular, pentagonal and quadrilateral signs whose surface is cut by a vertical median line. These broad signs present distinct regional differences: they are tectiform in Les Eyzies region, aviform in Quercy, quadrilateral at Lascaux and in Cantabria, and there are numerous variations on the theoretical model. In several cases we find no geometric signs but female sex symbols which show progressive degrees of geometricisation and which permit the identification of the extremes of this geometricisation process. In those caves where the figures are numerous and in different styles, for example at El Castillo, we may find broad signs of several more or less realistic types. One particular category of broad sign is that of the claviform signs, derived from the profile of a female figure. For these signs too, the morphological transformations are numerous, from the female silhouettes at Pech-Merle to the hundreds of engraved figures at Gönnersdorf. The claviform sign is found in two geographically distant zones, Ariège and Cantabro-Asturian Spain.

120. 122
106
107
108. 109
47

The third category of signs (S3) comprises black or red dots whose diameter varies from a few millimetres to 10 centimetres and more, and dashes, engraved or painted according to the circumstances. Their significance is far from clear, and they must have represented different concepts according to their number and disposition. On engraved blocks in the Aurignacian the dots accompany realistic female symbols in aligned rows. In the caves, one can cite two examples of single red spots, on the shoulder of a bison at Niaux and on a bison at Le Portel. But the most frequent case is that of lines of 4 to more than 20 dots above a cervico-dorsal line or between an animal's feet, for example the bison at Mas-d'Azil and at Bedeilhac, the aurochs and horse at La Pasiega, and the horse and stag at Lascaux. The second category of dots, aligned or grouped, mark in many caves the deep parts (terminal cul de sac or the beginning of a sequence), as at Lascaux, Le Portel and El Castillo. At Lascaux, particularly, the three terminals of the Axial Passage, the Shaft and the Chamber of the Felines are marked by lines or spreads of dots. We should point out the unique case of the bison at the furthest end of the large painted panel at Marsoulas, which is entirely made up of rows of tiny dots.

93. 98

The significant elements and the role of the parietal signs are still imperfectly understood. The relationship of signs to each other, their isolation in relation to animals, or, on the other hand, their juxtaposition or superimposition, implies the existence of a symbolic language whose pertinent traits for the most part escape us in the absence of an oral content. But before attempting a synthesis on 'the' cave, it is necessary to refer briefly to two categories of figures which could play a considerable part in the syntactical articulation: wounds and hands.

Wounds

Wounds are represented by a V sign, which may have a central shaft of varying length; this shaft could be the shaft of the spear or simply a line expressing the importance of the flow of blood escaping from the wound. This wound sign has provided the basis for the hypothesis, thought likely on other grounds, of practices of sympathetic magic on the figures of animals and even men.

56

Certain anomalies suggest that the problem is not entirely resolved by this hypothesis. Our hesitation in accepting unreservedly that animal figures were used as magic targets by hunters is because this role cannot be demonstrated, for the number of wounded animals is no more than 4% of the total number of animals represented. Their overall frequency varies according to the species: bison and aurochs around 8%, horse 2.5%, ibex and mammoth less than 1%. To these quantitative differences are added clear regional ones. The Charente–Périgord region has 0.65% of horses wounded (2 out of 307) and 3% of bison (2 out of 150); Quercy has no horses wounded out of 8, and 2 bisons out of 14; the Pyrenees has 10.8% of horses (15 out of 141) and 14% of bisons (35 out of 245); and Atlantic Spain has 1.3% of horses (2 out of 148) and 0.9% of bisons (1 out of 107). It seems clear that the bison, and to a lesser degree the horse, are the bearers of wounds and that geographically it is the Pyrenees (particularly in the Ariège region) where the great majority of cases are concentrated (Niaux, Le Portel, Bedeilhac, Montespan, Les Trois-Frères and Le Tuc-d'Audoubert, Fontanet). The walls of the Salon Noir at Niaux are so easily read that there is no scope for error; with a rate of 25% of animals wounded (18 out of 71) they reach the maximum among known examples.

74

This review of the problem of wounded animals only resolves some of the questions posed, but it has thrown up some probabilities. First of all, it confirms that, although it is difficult to defend the theory of sympathetic magic on game, the hunting symbolism of the concepts to which allusion is made is certain. What appears as even more striking is the concentration in the Pyrenees, where the number of animals wounded can reach up to 25% of the total while the rest of western Europe has hardly more than isolated cases. Wounding could perhaps be an animation theme of the same type as the animal sniffing the ground (reindeer at Limeuil), marking territory (bisons at Altamira) and emitting a breath (aurochs at Pech-Merle and feline at Lascaux). These inequalities, which are as much quantitative as qualitative, demonstrate the importance of the provincial facies, and certainly also the importance of the chronological periods in the variations in content of the figures.

122. 125

Hands

The hands are divided into two well-defined categories: hands with severed fingers and complete hands. The application of hands loaded with colour, or *positive* hands, are much more rare than *negative* hands which clearly show the silhouette in reserve on a splash of colour, usually red or black. In both categories, the first (mutilated hands) or the second (complete hands) they are only present in a few sites.

111

The cave at Gargas and its modest companion at Tibiran, a few hundred metres away, contain many negative hands (150+) in red ochre and black. These hands have as a peculiarity the absence of certain fingers, which for a single hand may range from any one finger to all bar the thumb. Various hypotheses have been put forward to explain this, which fall into two categories: ritual amputation or pathology. Religious amputation seems absurd, for one knows of no human group, particularly of hunters, who could consider the stump of a hand to be more advantageous in the chase than five intact fingers. The second hypothesis is that of the loss of the fingers through frostbite or illness and several mutilating diseases have been suggested, but Luquet, since 1926, has put forward the hypothesis that the fingers were certainly not mutilated but were bent for unknown reasons. If one seeks out a definition of the relationships between the different digital combinations, the repetition in groups of the same formulas and the distribution of colours, one reaches a perception of a code based on the transposition of hunting gestures designed for silent communication between hunters about the nature of the game, a code still practised by South African bushmen. On the other hand, in Spain, in the cave at Maltravieso, there are negative hands whose fifth finger-tip was amputated. Amputation of this kind, of little functional importance, can be found in a few regions of Oceania.

There seems to be no relationship between the Gargas and Tibiran hands and the other negative hands which occur in small numbers in other regions. In Périgord they are found at Font-de-Gaume, Bernifal and Les Combarelles, isolated or in very small numbers; in Quercy we find them at Pech-Merle, Les Fieux and Rocamadour. The cave at Rocamadour conceals a number of very curious hands with tapered fingers and retouched by scratching. In Cantabrian Spain complete hands can be seen at El Castillo.

110. 132

Whatever parts of the caves they are in, negative hands do not have a significant distribution. At Bernifal they are near the entrance, at El Castillo they are at the back, at Pech-Merle they are found around the dappled horses and at the entrance to the Passage with the women-bison, at Roucadour they are in the middle of the animals. They do not seem to have been topographically consistent, or at least their small number and their distribution does not permit one to assign to them a precise significance.

THE CAVE

The cave itself, as a whole or in certain parts, played in many cases the role of the female symbol. In fact one comes across natural irregularities in the walls like an oval niche (Font-de-Gaume) or a fissure (Niaux), or stalactites in the form of breasts (Le Combel at Pech-Merle) which gave rise to a comparison with female symbols. Signs with male connotations may, then, prove to be linked with natural features (Niaux, deep gallery). There is no doubt that certain parts of the cave acquired a sexual connotation on the part of palaeolithic man, but it is difficult to say to what extent the entire cave was thought of as 'the entrails of the earth'. One thing also certain is that parietal and mobiliary works covered the walls and floors of rock shelters which were lit by daylight, and the hundreds of plaques, rocks or fragments of bone material bear engravings which can also be found in open-air settlements far from the caves, showing that the ideological framework of the works was not exclusively linked to the cave. Moreover, the first examples of art, the engraved or painted blocks of the Aurignacian, do not seem to have had an equivalent in cave art apart from a few works difficult to date and anyway situated at the entrance, still in daylight (Les Bernous, for example).

112. 113
132

Knowledge of the deep parts of caves seems to have been progressively acquired. The speleological exploits of palaeolithic artists are surprising, however. We know that they had means of illumination in the form of stone lamps filled with grease, with juniper sprigs for wicks, and that their lighting capacity was satisfactory (*Lascaux inconnu* 1979), but they must have needed periodic refilling and above all relighting if they blew out. It is difficult to imagine a groping return from the far end of La Cullalvera (1500 metres through a pile of gigantic blocks) or Rouffignac (one kilometre through hundreds of bears' dens of caves) or even Niaux (1500 metres with multiple side passages). The remote parts of some of the caves seem only to have been visited once for the execution of the artworks, or at any rate only to have been very rarely visited. One cannot make a general rule from this observation, and yet works on remote walls do seem to leave the impression of an exceptional exploit. This is the case at Niaux where the mass of figures in the Salon Noir (already nearly a kilometre from the entrance) extends into two galleries where the figures spread out, isolated, over several hundred metres to reach the end drawings (two horses in the branch towards Lombrives and a horse, three bisons and a small carnivore in the branch off the Cartailhac gallery). All these figures are executed with an economy of colouring which limits the lines to the minimum that allows identification.

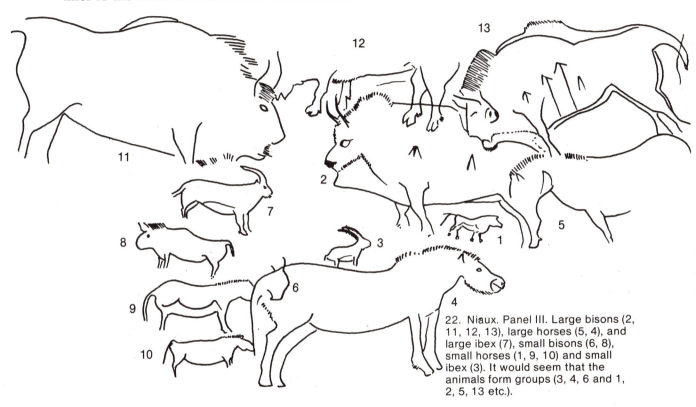

22. Niaux. Panel III. Large bisons (2, 11, 12, 13), large horses (5, 4), and large ibex (7), small bisons (6, 8), small horses (1, 9, 10) and small ibex (3). It would seem that the animals form groups (3, 4, 6 and 1, 2, 5, 13 etc.).

In the majority of decorated caves the figures are situated either in the well-lit entrance area or at depths no greater than a few dozen metres. Some of the caves are not easy of access as far as one can see, and where the palaeolithic ground surface did not undergo any modification they must have offered a long and difficult crawl, a hundred metres at Arcy-sur-Cure, for example, and formidable obstacles at Etcheberriko Kharbia.

Where the present entrance allows a reconstruction of what the palaeolithic entrance was like, it seems that the works were begun at the furthest point reached by sunlight. This is notably the case at Labastide and La Cullalvera. It is difficult to say whether the decorated caves were intensively visited or whether they were dealt with once and for all. A good number of them have additions or assemblages which suggest a return on two or more occasions, a few centuries or even several millennia apart. This does not imply a high rate of frequentation. Some caves, on the other hand, contain a profusion of figures which is hardly compatible with execution at a single time. Les Combarelles, for example, contains an assemblage made up of successive masses of superimposed drawings. The wall is somehow saturated over some 150 metres constituting the area covered with engravings, all of which belong to Style IV. The same thing is seen in the cave at Les Trois-Frères, where hundreds of small engravings are mixed up on the panels of the 'Sanctuary' below the composite figure of the 'Sorcerer'.

At first sight there seems to be no order ruling these innumerable figures, but comparison panel by panel leads quickly to the realisation that there is a spatial organisation, undefined but recognisable all the same. The domination of bison in number and size is striking in some of the panels, with grouped horses in the minority, ibexes inserted towards the edge, and a rhinoceros or the face of a feline on the outside. In another panel reindeer predominate, accompanied by a few horses or bisons. The horses themselves are in the majority in size and number in another panel, accompanied by small bisons and bears. These subtle variations recall those of the different panels at Niaux, in particular Panel III, where horses, bisons and ibexes change their relative size from one part of the panel to another. Niaux is not far from Les Trois-Frères, only 40 kilometres as the crow flies, and the two caves share with Le Portel the claviform signs that might be considered as the indicator of an ideology common to different ethnic groups who probably inhabited the Ariège region over a period of several centuries. From one cave to another, horse and bison apparently assume different relationships, but ultimately they derive from a common origin. The horses and bisons at Niaux take on relationships of dimension which give the two animals in turn alternating roles, and the ibex participates in this process. At Les Trois-Frères they are grouped in assemblages of horse–bison–reindeer in which the ibex plays a relatively marginal role. One also finds the 'dimension' factor in the two panels on which the flood of tangled figures only allows the head and the ends of the hooves of a very large bison to appear. This distribution of animals which take the dominant role in turn through their size and, on the other hand, the existence of a system of panels on which can be seen the quantitative pre-eminence of one species in distinct topographic fields helps in the comprehension of the distribution of figures at Le Portel. There the 'dimension' element does not seem to have played any role but, instead, topographic selectivity has particularly marked characteristics. The cave is made up of four galleries. Gallery II contains different assemblages of horses, bisons, ibexes, stags and men, the whole complex earlier than the contents of galleries III and IV whose figures are all in Style IV and therefore presumed to be Middle and Late Magdalenian. In gallery III the ensemble is made up of eleven horses and a single bison, while gallery IV contains ten bisons and a single painted horse.

Le Portel was the first cave that led me to formulate the hypothesis of the opposition and complementarity of the horse and the bison, a hypothesis which came to confirm that which Annette Laming-Emperaire formed at Lascaux on the special relationship of the horse–aurochs pair. The metaphysical alternation of the horse and the bison cannot be better expressed than in these two groups of paintings each exchanging one of its symbols for one of the other's. The risks of an explanation are always great, and it does not seem possible at the present time to suggest anything other than this fundamental liaison between animals (horse–bison) which alternate, having as possible partner the ibex (Le Portel, Niaux, Les Trois-Frères); the stag is quantitatively secondary and is in a lateral position. Conformity to the A–B–C model can be seen in a very clear way in the 'Camarin' at Le Portel, an alcove in which the bison and the horse are in the central position, flanked on the left by an ibex and on the right margin by a stag's antlers. The spatial relationships are the same in the three caves. At Niaux the ibexes are peripheral to the bisons in Panel I; in Panel II on the upper margin two ibexes frame a bison on the pediment; in Panel III there are two ibexes, one below a bison, the other, very small, on the back of the main horse; in Panel IV there is one under the belly of a bison. This positioning of the ibex is found in various forms at Pair-non-Pair, La Mouthe (Panel II) and Ekaïn. At Lascaux: first, the ibexes in the Axial Passage are situated towards the back, on the margin of the aurochs and horse assemblages;

23

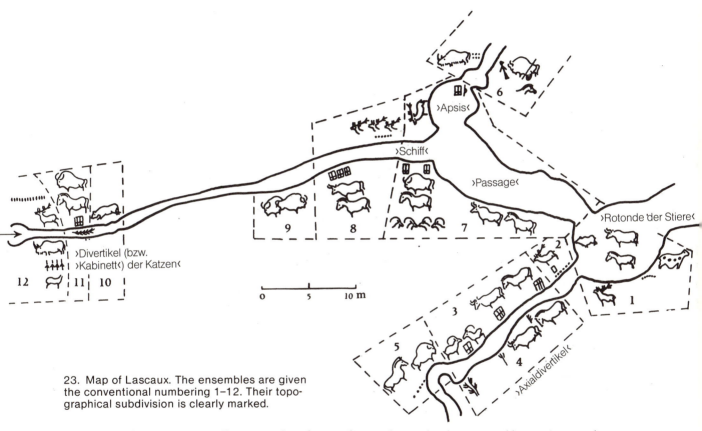

23. Map of Lascaux. The ensembles are given the conventional numbering 1–12. Their topographical subdivision is clearly marked.

second, at the entrance to the Nave they form a frieze above the 'horses and bisons' group known as the 'Empreinte'; third, a last group of ibexes are found on the edge of the feline assemblage. The ibex appears in an even more marginal situation when it is isolated in a nook, as at Pech-Merle, or at the entrance to a passage, as at El Castillo or La Pasiega, or again among the furthest figures in a recess (El Castillo, La Pasiega). This latter position associates it with back-cave cervids (Altamira, La Pasiega C and El Castillo), with which it is in a position of concurrence. In Lascaux, at the entrance and at the end of the Axial Passage, it seems that the ibex is rather more marginally localised within the central assemblage of A–B horse–bovine, than is evident at Niaux. The stag is apparently even more marginal, located as it is on the two edges towards the entrance and towards the back. It is an animal which frames the areas occupied by horses and bovines, as at Lascaux. The Covalanas ensemble is unusual in this regard: fifteen hinds spread out on the two walls frame an aurochs head and a horse, one on each wall. At Altamira, El Castillo and Pindal, in the Cantabrian province, a third animal is added to the ibex or the stag, and occasionally to both. This is the mammoth, one single individual in each of the three caves, all three allied to Style IV. These mammoths are situated in the furthest part of the deep gallery and turn their heads towards the back. It is interesting to note in passing that this situation is not known elsewhere, and that in Aquitaine the rhinoceros is in a homologous position to that of the Cantabrian mammoth (for example Lascaux and Font-de-Gaume). For as yet unknown reasons, but not necessarily climatic, the reindeer too is more southerly than expected, being found from the Basque country as far as Asturia (Altxerri, Las Monedas, Tito Bustillo).

Significant space

The systematic analysis of assemblages of figures is made difficult by the many micro-topographic variations which link the work and its support, although one can perceive a common orientation. From the outset, the Aurignacian blocks at La Ferrassie expressed in sex symbols what one thinks of as objects of a 'fertility cult'; strictly speaking this is not very informative, since more or less all 'cults' have fertility as one of their preoccupations. The engraved blocks from the Les Eyzies region (Abri Blanchard, Castanet, Cellier) are evidence of this fact. The problem, however, is not there; it lies in the presence from the start of incisions and of lines of dots for which there is no satisfactory interpretation. Simultaneously the first images of animals appeared, which apparently reflects the exercise of 'hunting magic'. That must have been a very useful discovery in the heroic period of the pioneers of prehistoric research, but it had no more originality than the fertility cult. Let us admit right away that palaeolithic man practised a general fertility cult through magic rites for both man and animal, except perhaps for bear, lion and rhinoceros. With these foundations laid there still remains a considerable residue of subjects for study. First of all there is the artistic analysis of the work, an area which has not yet been much investigated. Almost everything still remains to be said about the actual techniques of engraving, painting and sculpture. It is only very recently that there has even been any serious interest in the nature of the colouring materials with which the paintings were executed. It has emerged that the yellows, reds, browns and blacks are of a more complex mineralogical or organic (charcoal) origin than has been hitherto supposed. It is difficult to unravel the question of styles without a thorough understanding of the characteristics which may only reflect restraints of a technical nature. With these last at least recognised if not mastered, we are faced with problems of craft in its true sense, which are reduced to the representation of time and space. The quest for a translation of real space into wall space marks the evolution of the pictorial process, and the steps taken can be measured through the rendering of figures at rest or in movement. All the works are far from being perfect in their execution, but the very great majority demonstrate an exercise born of long practice, giving valuable indirect information on social structure. In another direction there is still much to be learnt about the symbolic value of the figures, in particular about the coexistence of realistic and geometric subjects. Independently of the actual meaning of these geometric figures, this unusual procedure is strongly characteristic of parietal art. The fact is all the more curious because the evolution of

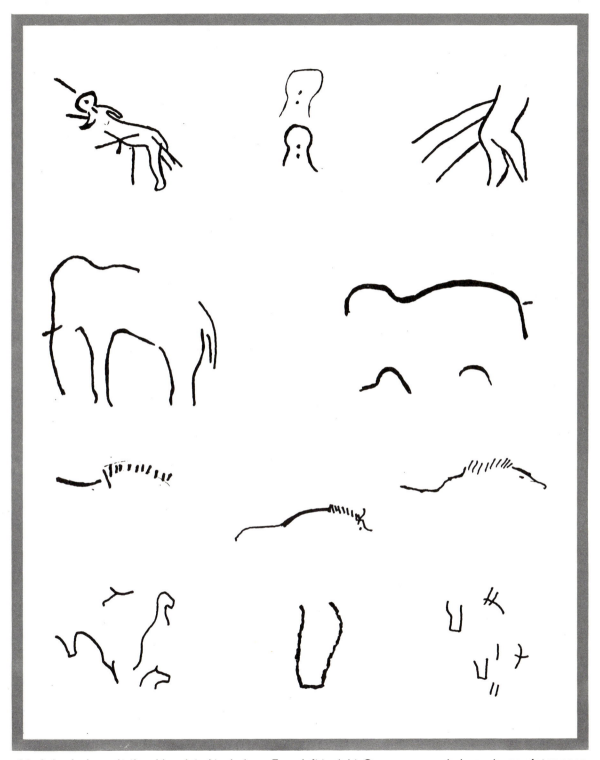

24. Animals drawn in the abbreviated technique. From left to right: Cougnac, wounded man, human faces seen from the front, wounded man. Mammoth, three abbreviated cervico-dorsal lines of a mammoth. Mane and dorsal line of a horse (Cougnac), a bison (Niaux) and another horse (Niaux). Bovine, feline, horse (head and shoulders) (Bayol); very synthetic horse's head; graffito representing two horses and probably horned animals (bison and aurochs) (Bayol).

geometric symbols of animal origin in mobiliary art does not apparently represent the same ideological process, for the mobiliary signs are rare on the walls and the parietal broad signs are virtually absent on mobiliary works.

It is possible that the mobiliary and parietal lines of evolution arise from very different motivations. That of mobiliary art is apparently linked to the precarious nature of the objects on which it is found, like spear-points which are quickly broken or lost. Independently of all metaphysical interpretation, the normal routes of geometricisation led, for mobiliary subjects, towards the repetitive drawing of triangles, zig-zags or oval shapes. On the other hand, geometric evolution of parietal figures could have been motivated by the symbolism of signs with male and female connotations and following a development towards complexity for perhaps esoteric reasons – at any rate different in their nature from those used to decorate objects. But another

24   evolutionary process is possible for the parietal animal figures, and that is *abbreviation* which is based on completely different principles from those of geometricisation – the pursuit of the minimum number of traits necessary to ensure the identification of the animal. Some of the

114   figures at Niaux illustrate the process well, for example the branched sign and horse in the deep gallery and the bisons and horse in the Clastres gallery. An 'economic' motive probably explains these unfinished lines, for their very remote position, more than a kilometre from the entrance, could have imposed both a reduction to the minimum of the time for execution and a need to spare paints and lights. But abbreviation is also found in relatively accessible caves, for example at

115   Cougnac, where, in the open areas within the outline of a deer with giant antlers (Megaceros), there is a mammoth limited to the frontal dome and the back, a stag minimally drawn, and a man pierced with spears limited to the torso and legs. The type of abbreviation at Cougnac is identical

116   with that of two of the figures at Pech-Merle, a nearby and contemporary cave: these are the aurochs and the stag in the niches behind the 'women–bison' cave, in the area near the wounded man and the single ibex. The motives for these figures remain obscure, but without questioning the foundations of palaeolithic religion, one might think that it was economic motives, again, which persuaded the artists to give to peripheral images the minimum desirable identity.

On the eastern periphery of the Franco-Cantabrian area, a few caves, notably La Baume d'Oullen (Ardèche) and Bayol (Gard), show an evolutionary phenomenon of a very interesting nature. At Cullen, the mammoth is rendered by the cranial and dorsal bosses, and the ibex by a line in which only the two horns suggest the identification, the rest of the lines being unintelligible. The signs too have undergone a very obvious abbreviation. The Bayol cave contains some very odd figures: no subject is represented by anything other than the head, except the ibex at the entrance (which is in synthetic figurative and on the verge of being geometric) and the feline in the largest of the panels. This feline is drawn with a single line running from the nose and indicating with undulations the head, the back and the tail. Along with La Baume Latrone it is the only known example of such a figure. Unfortunately, in the absence of possible comparisons, it has not been possible to date these original monuments with precision. It is even more regrettable in the knowledge that these two caves have been plundered over a long period of years and that almost nothing visible remains. It is also regrettable because, in graphic terms, the Bayol figures correspond to an evolution parallel with that of several scripts where whole figures are progressively resolved by abbreviation into ideograms. It is in no way legitimate to see in this writing in its real or commonplace sense, but the same point is reached here where signs of

25. Broad signs found in various regions. 1–4: quadrilaterals, Perigord. 5–12 true and characteristic tectiform signs. 13 and 14 claviforms. 19–26 quadrilaterals of Cantabrian derivation. 27 and 28 Cantabrian quadrilaterals, Altamira.

ideographic character serve as pointers to the revelation of an oral tradition. The extreme graphic austerity of these south-eastern palaeolithic men is certainly evidence of importance. Even the most rough evidence for communication is immensely valuable for the comprehension of palaeolithic art, and beyond that for art in general. The impression of the whole puts palaeolithic works into the category of mythograms, that is to say of symbolic figures without reference to coordinated time and space, whose relationship to the subject is not part of a narrative structure other than oral. As in numerous cases of arts which have justly been called 'primitive', the actors are drawn and set opposite each other in a space with no guiding line. It is the absence of linearity which gives the mythogram its character – the elements are not aligned as in a cartoon or a text, or linked up by a line of footprints as in the codices of precolumbian Mexico. If we think of the figures as elements significant in their ensemble, they do not express determined action. At first sight, with no indication of a role made material by descriptive attitudes or movements and without spatio-temporal links, the assemblages allow little room for an elaborate interpretation. Even in the absence of linearity, however, there remains a certain balance between the figures and in relation to the parietal support. This is why it is important to seek out the indices of composition which can reveal the integration of the images in their own spatial (symmetry, perspective) and temporal (animation) context.

25 *The signs.* In regard to space, the signs forming a cross in the cave at El Castillo make a very illuminating example. In a broad passage off the main gallery in the cave, a dozen large quadrilateral signs intersected by alignments of dots grouped in four parallel rows are painted in red on part of the ceiling. These signs are very common in El Castillo and other caves in the area, including Altamira; the quadrilaterals are included in the class of broad signs and the lines of dots in that of narrow signs. Now a unique occurrence in what we know of palaeolithic art is that on the other half of the ceiling there are two quadrilaterals forming a cross at one end and two bands of dots, also crossed, at the other. It is very clear that the meaning of this assemblage may for ever elude us, but we can say with certainty that at one time it meant something, as did the dozen aligned signs opposite it and the grouping of all these signs in a passage which contains nothing else. Because of their regional character, in a territory which to the present day hardly exceeds thirty kilometres, these signs correspond to a Franco-Iberian model for which there are other regional equivalents from the Loire to not far from Gibralter. The signs provide several very good examples suitable for extracting the original ethnic character of each of the groups detectable through the variations. This leads us to a first logical conclusion: on the one hand, there is an underlying cultural unity of the different human groups scattered across Europe, a unity which suggests the circulation of traditions on a vast scale in time and space; on the other, each of the regional groups has a well-marked character, implying a sufficiently prolonged development on the same territory for the different peoples who frequented it to become clearly distinguished. The esoteric signs in the caves are perhaps more suitable than the animal figures for studying the unity and the diversity of palaeolithic art.

The animals. The principal participants have already been enumerated, and to a certain extent we have seen that listing them in quantitative groups demonstrates the selective nature of their presence and their location. We have seen that horses and bovines were the hosts of the open areas of the walls, as principal elements in the panels. These three animals (horse, bison, aurochs) comprise by themselves around 60% of the animal figures. A second group of around 30% follow, including stag and hind, mammoth, ibex and reindeer, which we have designated 'complementary animals'. The rest of the animals share the remaining 10%: feline, bear and rhinoceros, with a few very rare species such as the boars from Altamira (often disputed), the nocturnal predators of Le Portel and Les Trois-Frères, the Isturitz crow, a few fish and a few monsters. How are these signs and animals qualitatively and quantitatively organised?

To answer this question it is necessary to start by considering the setting in which these actors appear. Each decorated cave has its own shape, resulting from the effects of subterranean erosion and concretion. These morphological factors underlie many different shapes which can be simplified down to a few main types:

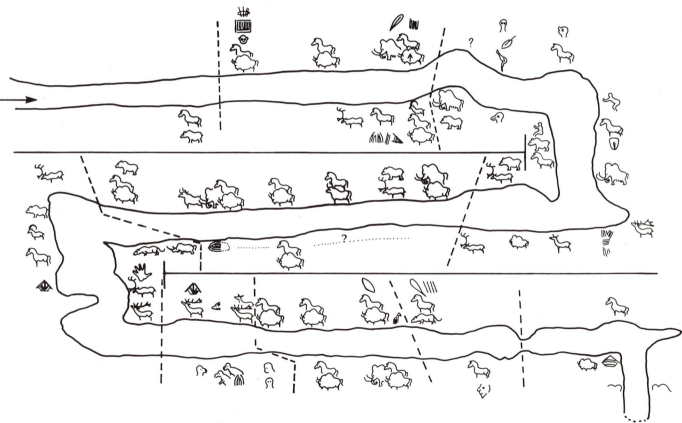

26. Les Combarelles. Schematic map and conventionalised representation of the different assemblages. Despite their complexity the figures from Les Combarelles constitute one of the best examples of topographic organisation. The legibility is due to the very structure of the cave: a long passage with well-defined divisions.

(1) Broad areas of wall suitable for the painting of many figures, in particular the ceiling surfaces, like the famous ceiling at Altamira and those of Rouffignac and Ekaĩn, or the surfaces with multiple planes, like Niaux (Salon Noir) or Les Trois-Frères 'sanctuary'.

(2) Vertical surfaces in galleries suitable for the unrolling of a register of figures of various length. The artist was invited to align his works horizontally, as in the corridor at Les Combarelles or Le Gabillou, Font-de-Gaume, Santimamiñe and Pindal.

Some caves offer both possibilities, for example Rouffignac, Altamira, Ebbou and Pech-Merle (dappled horses and particularly the Black Frieze).

(3) Natural features, which limit the extent of the panels, determined by the state of the rock (fissures, stratification joints), by the action of erosion (defining the boundaries of a free surface, usually concave), or by concretion (stalactites, stalagmites and folds). Each cave has its own features which could have influenced the choice of figure placings and which often limited the assemblages.

THE EARLIEST EVIDENCE

We have seen above that the earliest examples we know of are the Aurignacian blocks of the Les Eyzies region (c. 30,000 BC) and that the parietal sites going back to the same period are earlier than the cave paintings. It is hard to tell if these blocks were disposed in a meaningful way: proofs of the existence of a model assemblage are later (Perigordian or Late Aurignacian, 25,000–15,000 BC). The sites which pose the problem of archaic parietal art are Pair-non-Pair (Gironde) Gargas (Haute-Pyrenées), Roucadour (Lot) and Les Bernous (Dordogne). Les Bernous contains, at the entrance, three silhouettes in bas-relief: one of a recognisable mammoth; and two figures which could pass for a rhinoceros and a bear, though no certainty is possible; no information was available from the remains which might have been found in the soil beneath the figures. Roucadour has not yet been the object of a detailed study, but we know of some fine engravings there of horses, bisons and ibexes associated with broad circular signs not unlike the signs at Pair-non-Pair. The outlines of the engraved animals from Roucadour have close affinities with the animals from Gargas ('La Conque') and Pair-non-Pair. La Conque at Gargas is a small panel on which appear essentially a bovine head facing left, a horse head facing right, crossing the bovine, and a small mammoth outline. We shall see below that this group constitutes an assemblage of the ordinary A–B–C type, that is horse–bovine–mammoth. It is difficult to say whether the small size of the mammoth and its lateral position are significant. The deep position of the figures in the cave contradicts the presumed position of the earliest figures, but it can still be established today that daylight reflected by the wall permitted, in case of need, return without a light. Consideration of the figures at Pair-non-Pair confirms some of the observations made at Gargas. The decoration comprises six panels in all. The main assemblage (panels 1 and 2) is made up of three registers, the bottom with two horses in line, the middle with two confronting bovines and a mammoth, and the top with five ibexes. The topographic formula is as follows:

$$CCCCC^3$$
$$B\text{--}B + C^2$$
$$A\text{--}A$$

identical to the one at Gargas (A–B + C), A–B constituting the central assemblage (corresponding with its situation in almost all cases) while C (which can be a stag, a hind, an ibex, a mammoth or a reindeer) plays an important but not obligatory role, that is, it can be absent, leaving the A–B group on its own (Marcenac, La Madeleine). At this last site the horse and bison face each other on opposite walls as at Marcenac, but with an elongated female figure next to each. Animal C can be missing, but it is normally represented by at least one of the five animals in the category.

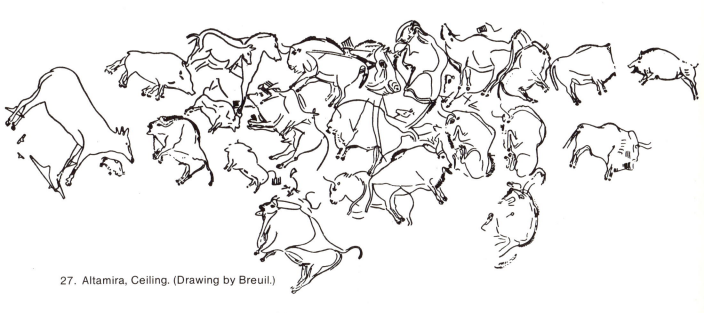

27. Altamira, Ceiling. (Drawing by Breuil.)

THE LARGE PANELS

The panels have several registers; in other words those ceilings or open walls where there is sufficient space to fit in several figures vertically are particularly suitable for extracting this complex organisation. The painted ceiling at Altamira can be read in this way:

$$
\begin{array}{ccc}
\text{A} & \text{A} & \text{D} \\
\text{C}^{1b}\text{C}^{1b}\text{B}^1 & \text{B}^1\ \text{B}^1\ \text{B}^1\ \text{B}^1 & \\
\text{C}^3 & \text{B}^1\ \text{B}^1\ \text{B}^1\ \text{B}^1\ \text{B}^1\ \text{B}^1\ \text{B}^1 & \\
\text{C}^{1b}\text{C}^3 & \text{B}^1\ \text{B}^1\ \text{B}^1\ \text{B}^1\ \text{B}^1\ \text{B}^1 &
\end{array}
$$

Two horses can be seen here, one at the top of the central axis and represented with an enormous head. The majority of the ceiling surface is covered with the images of 17 bisons. This spread of bisons (B^1) is bordered with a boar (D), the two horses (A) and the two hinds (C^{1b}). The horses are present, but in a marginal position. To be noticed in passing as perhaps significant are the large horse's head which dominates the ceiling assemblage, and the little bison on the edge under the neck of the hind. This disposition is reminiscent of the play in dimensions between the horse, the bison and the ibex at Niaux, contemporary but on the other side of the Pyrenees.

To validate Altamira, there is an exactly inverse assemblage at Ekaïn, 150 kilometres from

69

28. Ekaïn. Large panel.

28 Altamira, where the horse is numerically dominant. The cave contains three principal assemblages, two of them made up of linear series. The third is on a ceiling surface and depicts the elements of the following formula:

$$C^1$$

$$B? \ B^1 \ \underline{B^1} \ B^1$$

$$C^3 \quad A \ A \ A \ \underline{A}$$

$$A \quad A \ A \ A$$

$$A \ A$$

$$P$$

(fish)

70

It is the horses which star in this version of the assemblage which we must regard as significant, all the more because the two principal actors, the underlined bison and horse, are the only figures in the whole ensemble to be highlighted in red ochre. The two group C figures, ibex (C^3) and hind (C^{1b}), and the fish (P) are all distributed on the periphery.

A final example of a formula for an assemblage is that to be found in the alcove at Le Portel, named by H. Breuil the 'Camarin':

$$A$$
$$C^3 \ B^1 \ C^1$$

The group C animals are, as always, marginal. The ibex, which is represented almost entirely, is better integrated than the stag which is reduced to its antlers. This marginal but slightly different situation is something that we can see at Niaux, another site belonging to the Ariège group.

The clearest, perhaps because it assembles many animals in various situations, is the Rouffignac ceiling. The list of animals present is exhaustive in relation to the cave ensemble: horse (7A) and bison (9B) – mammoth (16 C^2), ibex (11 C^3) and rhinoceros (3 D^3). The 16 animals of groups A–B share the first accessible surface coming from daylight, and form three groups, one of six horses, the other two of 5 and 4 bisons respectively framing the six central horses. If one demarcates the continuous surface occupied by each of the five species represented one can see that each constitutes a coherent topographic group, the horses and bisons, already considered, and the mammoths and ibexes in two groups occupying the most distant surround of the ceiling, in a position analogous to that at Ekaïn, Niaux and Altamira (central and peripheral figures). But another aspect of the ensemble is apparent: the sizes of the different figures are probably significant, for the four largest figures are a bison restricted to its head (like the principal horse at Altamira), a horse, a mammoth, all in the central space, and an ibex on the furthest margin. To this peculiarity is added the fact that the interplay of species is almost as apparent as in panel III at Niaux: small mammoth near large horse, small horse behind large mammoth, small bison in the neighbourhood of a group of mammoths and another near the ibex. This exchange of species in which one is always subordinate reflects metaphysical and social concepts that are still difficult to fathom. Les Trois-Frères sanctuary, with its panels where we find the same species of animals but where each time one of them (bison, horse or reindeer) is privileged in number and size, suggests an organisation of the same type. Another uncommon trait on the great ceiling at Rouffignac is the presence of three rhinoceroses, one in the first group of bisons, one on the opposite margin to the first, and the third among the ibexes.

At Les Trois-Frères, the rhinoceros appears on the edge of one of the panels, the only representative of its species, and the mammoth too is in a marginal and unique position; at Niaux both species are totally absent. At Rouffignac on the other hand, the mammoth dominates considerably. I think that this in no way alters the visibility of the A–B–C model. The variations on the basic formula, like the broad signs, could have marked ethnic and chronologically different entities. At Covalanas near Santander, the formula is made up of a horse (A), an aurochs head (B) and 17 hinds (C^{1b}). At Pech-Merle, among the figures in the Black Frieze, aurochs, bison and mammoth are in the majority with the horses reduced to three individuals.

22

CAVES AND SHELTERS WITH LINEAR WALLS

This is the most common case: instead of being able to spread in all directions, the available area is in the form of a band or a sequence of little panels. This situation is predominant for the sculpted friezes under the Mouthiers shelter and those at Le Roc-de-Sers and Le Cap Blanc, as well as for the corridor-caves like Les Combarelles and Le Gabillou; but in the majority of cases the decorated ensemble is made up of surfaces of infinitely variable shape, contriving to produce a run of variable length. These conditions would appear to favour the development of a less mythographic structure than the panels, for the entry into successive scenes of different actors would produce a pictographic series comparable to a strip cartoon. Experience proves that palaeolithic men projected essentially mythographic images onto their walls. In fact we are not dealing with an unfolding but rather a building-up of an assemblage with a central space and peripheral areas. The figures are not linked together but are juxtaposed or superimposed in a space that could be compared to the curve of a bell, with the bovine occupying the summit and the horse, in a considerable number of cases and although the central animal, subordinate in both position and size to the bovine image: Le Gabillou, Niaux (Panel II), Lascaux (Axial Passage, Hall of the Bulls, 'Empreinte', cow in the Nave, Passage of the Felines); while the complementary animals may be found on all the margins of the imaginary curve. This scheme takes up again the main lines of the model whose development we have seen on ceiling surfaces or walls of vast proportions. When we consider the swarming of images on the walls of Les Combarelles, we perceive:

26

(1) that the bovines, bisons and aurochs, are situated in the rectilinear areas, in more or less the central part of each of the three galleries according to the state of the wall. No bovine is found in the bends. This situation is the same as for the surfaces of large size, but the very numerous horses are situated in the same register as the bovines, as are also the animals of classes C and D (stags, mammoths, ibexes, reindeer, bears, felines and rhinoceroses).

(2) Thus the arrangement is not made up of a sequence of animals of all species, but the animals follow a deliberate distribution which is closely similar to that of the mythograms with multi-directional expansion.

It is in any case clear that where it is possible to insert an extra figure into the available height, it is generally the complementary animal, the ibex, that is to be found. An even more convincing fact is that the assemblages which appear to be a confused mass of superimposed figures are almost all centred on a large bison image. It is in these assemblages that we find the association of A–B + C animals in the form of horse and bison plus ibex, mammoth or reindeer. Of fifteen surfaces with superimposed figures, eleven are made up of a large bovine, one or more horses and one or more complementary animals. Superimposition really does seem to be as we suggested above, a figurative process peculiar to certain caves where the mobility of the artist was limited to the range of the manual field. We must not lose sight of the fact that in its original state Les Combarelles was only a narrow passage of varying steepness. These material reasons are clearly not the only ones concerned, but they did favour the grouping of figures in significant assemblages. Supplementary proof comes from the topographical position of bisons and aurochs in the long parts of the passage which has two hairpin bends. The eleven bovines, the cores of the assemblages of superimposed figures, are all in the long and relatively uncluttered areas, while the walls of the bends are peopled with horses (A), mammoths (C^4), stags (C^1), ibexes (C^3) and reindeer

(C^4) to the exclusion of all group B figures. So it seems likely that the elements of the mythogram were integrated into a double spatial organisation, each bovine forming the centre of a mythographic assemblage of the A–B + C D type (+ A–B + C D etc.), and the whole group of galleries taken as being superimposed according to the A–B + C–D model.

The organisation of the assemblages certainly seems to have been dictated to a large extent by the natural layout of the cave in which the works were done, but it is the mythogram which conditions the choice of topographical adaptation. Each cave is characterised in a particular manner: let us take sites like Font-de-Gaume, Bernifal, Les Combarelles and Rouffignac, which can be considered contemporary (contemporaneity for the prehistorian does not achieve rigorous synchronism, but it can define a homogeneous slice of time to about a few centuries) and of the same formula, $A–B^1 + C^2$, that is horse–bison + mammoth. In all four caves the mammoth is well represented, indeed at Rouffignac it is the quantitively predominant animal. In contrast the ibex is very modestly figured, and the rhinoceros is represented in three of the sites, but is absent at Bernifal. Each of the caves accords different possibilities which determine the distribution of the figures in each one. At Bernifal the walls are of mediocre quality and the figures are executed on restricted surfaces and on the smallest shelf without very obvious mythographic organisation. Les Combarelles, over a hundred metres long, has this device of animals focused on a dozen bisons spaced along a narrow but just about continuous wall. Font-de-Gaume is of more monumental proportions but is linear in structure like Les Combarelles. One does not, however, find so clearly there the arrangement by successive foci, but one sees long lines of bisons partially superimposed on mammoths and reindeer. The large bisons, between one and one and a half metres high, have dimensions double those of the Les Combarelles and Bernifal figures. A continuous ledge simulating a ground-surface line underlines this linearisation of the assemblages. Finally Rouffignac is of linear form in the galleries, the animals following each other in lines, like the three rhinoceroses or the eleven mammoths in two opposing groups. In contrast, the ceiling of the room of the gulf develops, over several tens of square metres, an important mythogram which was described above. Multi-directional in structure, Rouffignac is perhaps the best example, along with Les Combarelles, of the influence of the form of the walls on the presentation of the content of the assemblages.

The content of the message

Parietal palaeolithic art, like mobiliary art, brings to our attention considerable evidence for man's faunal environment, and numerous researchers have made use of the services which knowledge of the works can render to prehistoric research. In the bio-climatic area the parietal documents only prove one thing, that man knew the animals he drew, though we cannot say whether they existed in the region at the time the paintings were done, or whether those animals missing from the assemblages were too important or not important enough to figure on the walls. The rare evidence that we possess of bones and artworks together at the same site shows up significant gaps: why is there only one figure of a reindeer at Lascaux when its presence is almost exclusive among the bone debris, food remains which litter the floor of the cave? Why is the rhinoceros, which is present at Font-de-Gaume, Les Combarelles and Rouffignac, absent at Bernifal when the four caves have so many points in common? Why is the mammoth totally missing at Niaux and Le Portel when it is present at Les Trois-Frères? Why are animals marked with wounds at vital points only a small proportion of the figures when the practice of magic would have led one to suppose that all subjects would have been marked by the mortal sign? I think that it is often necessary to dissociate the wall and the ground below it. Too many prehistorians have seen in palaeolithic art (like a far-off predecessor of Egyptian or Etruscan tomb-painting) a sort of illustration of 'works and days'. Palaeolithic men could not have painted or engraved dances, hunts, funerary rituals or shamanistic circlings. This does not prove that they did not know of them or that they did not perform them at the foot of the figures. This suggestion admitted, numerous questions continue to arise, in particular those which touch on the deep meaning of the practices which drove them to place on the walls these hierarchically coordinated images of animals. Even if the occupation of the walls by the animal figures is relatively late, it supposes the preservation of the same archetype A–B + C over at least 5000 years. This is more time than any other known civilisation. If the symbolic formula has remained unchanged since the Aurignacian (30,000 BC), the length of its life reaches some twenty thousand years. But the endurance of the symbolic figures does not extend to meaning given to them, and this is the point that we must not lose sight of. If we take an example from a world which is familiar to us, the cross, for the Christian world, is a symbol that has endured for 2000 years: it can be considered as a highly significant symbol, but it does not prejudge either the doctrine or the liturgy, respectively 'upstream and downstream' of the figured subject. The Orthodox, Catholic, Protestant, Maronite, Coptic, Armenian, Ethiopian and Nestorian churches have a stock of figured symbols which are only intelligible within the circle of each of these churches. There is nothing to prevent the supposition that it was the same in the Palaeolithic. We know today that men who belong to cultures that we have considered 'primitive' can have symbolic systems of great complexity; the creators of the underground decorations must have had recourse to an iconography which linked the artists' image of the bestiary with the signs which were in some way geometricised. The articulation between these signs and the animals is still not very clear, for the signs sometimes occur grouped with the animal figures and sometimes isolated or grouped in a passage. The greatest difficulty in interpretation occurs when dealing with sites often separated by centuries and occasionally by considerable distances. It is particularly fortunate that objective links exist between certain geographically limited ensembles, such as the sites with tectiform signs and numerous mammoths in the Les Eyzies region (Bernifal, Les Combarelles, Font-de-Gaume and Rouffignac), or sites with quadrilateral signs in the Santander region (Castillo, Pasiega, Chimeneas, Altamira), or again the sites with claviform signs in the Ariège or Cantabrian regions. These facts tend to raise the question of considering the cave as a 'temple', that is, as a cult place accessible to all or at least a relatively large proportion of the community, while the sanctuary denotes a sacred place with access reserved for a minority. The sanctuary can be part of a temple. Can we imagine a crowd pressing up against the decorated walls and taking part in rituals? Lascaux would lead one to think so, with its incredible jumble of engravings in the Apse as well as the richness of the Hall of the Bulls, the Axial Passage and the Nave. It seems unlikely that the sumptuous decoration of the walls would have been reserved for one or two individuals: behind this decoration we can perceive the involvement of a whole community who maintained a few artists of high talent during the long weeks which they spent preparing the scaffolding, the colouring matter and the lighting. The time spent felling trees ten to fifteen centimetres in diameter for scaffolding, traces of which have been found, in procuring colours and grease to ensure lighting (more than 130 lamps have been found) represents a fairly considerable communal investment. Even if the paintings were executed in several stages, it implies an economic situation in which the group authorises surpluses to be expended in occupations of non-vital interest. One could remark that among populations at the stage of a hunting economy, the religious side is inseparable from the technological side and that it may have seemed essential to create these underground monuments, the decorated caves, in order to govern the physical world. And yet Lascaux, like Altamira or Niaux, are not only evidence of a magic activity linked to hunting, but are also, in view of the community involvement they suggest, evidence of a high cultural level of society which made the creative activity possible and, for the period of production, evidence of an economy capable of setting aside the means necessary for the realisation of masterpieces. Although it cannot be shown other than by indirect argument, Lascaux can be considered a temple. But all its parts are not as easily accessible, and not all bear traces of repeated visits: for example the Shaft and the Passage of the Felines where access is difficult and which might be considered sanctuaries. The execution of the Passage of the Felines, a narrow passage in practice limited to engraving, is of an austerity which contrasts with the sumptuousness of the decoration on the vast walls of the remainder of the cave. This contrast, between the walls covered with great works suggesting at least relatively frequent visiting and the walls of the deeper parts, can also be found at Altamira. There the monumental ceiling is almost at the entrance of the cave, the successive rooms offering painted decoration of modest character and leading to a narrow passage in which only engravings, though excellently done, are present.

It is not easy to place the parietal artist in his social role. It is possible that there were ethnic groups who more or less developed their artistic productions independently of the richness of their territories in hunting or fishing. In New Guinea the Papuans of the Sepik valley have an art of great quality reflected in the production of thousands of works. The people from neighbouring territories ignore almost everything in the artistic field. It is certain that some of our palaeolithic men achieved a mastery of form in engraving and painting which implies the existence of a great number of opportunities to practise it. We possess sufficient objects of mobiliary art to hold this hypothesis as proven, but alas nothing will bring back the painted bison-skins, the decorated bark, perhaps statues; perishable materials leave no trace in the soil for saying such things. Did the artist who appears in this evanescent form behind the works really exist? Was he a man gifted with talent who had an exceptional value in his group? Was he something else? A hunter among hunters who profited for a time from the material possibility of realising the underground images? Was he at the same time the author of the decoration and a participant in the esoteric knowledge, seen as a priest, a sort of shaman? It is quite clear that the status of the artist must have varied according to the groups and the periods, and that we must think of an execution which could, in some cases, have lasted more than a generation with its reworkings. Niaux or the painted works of Lascaux, the bas-reliefs of Angles-sur-l'Anglin or Le Cap Blanc were reworked sometimes to a considerable extent so that, in the absence of means of characterising the work of each painter or engraver, we can be all the more conscious, in front of these walls, of the reflection across 20,000 years of the fleeting silhouette of the oldest artist in the world.

Bibliography

Barandiaran, J-M de, 'Le cueva de Altxerri y sus figuras rupestres', *Munibe*, 16 (1964), 91–141.

Barandiaran, J-M de, and Altuna, J., 'La cueva de Ekaīn y sus figuras rupestres', *Munibe*, 1969 and 1980.

Breuil, H., *Quatre cents siècles d'art pariétal,* Montignac, Centre d'études et de documentation préhistoriques, 1952.

Giedion, S., *The eternal present: the beginnings of art. A contribution to constancy and change*, New York, Bollingen Foundation 1962 (Bollingen series XXXV, 6, 1).

Graziosi, P., *L'arte dell'antica età della pietra,* Florence, Sansoni, 1956.

Laming-Emperaire, A., *La signification de l'art rupestre paléolithique,* Paris, A. and J. Picard, 1962.

Leroi-Gourhan, A., *Préhistoire de l'art occidental,* Paris, Mazenod, 1965.

Leroi-Gourhan, A., *Les religions de la préhistoire*, Paris, Presses Universitaires de France, 1964.

Leroi-Gourhan, A. and Allain, J. *et al, Lascaux inconnu*, Paris CNRS, 1979 (XXe suppl. to *Gallia Préhistoire*).

Ucko, P.J. and Rosenfeld, A., *Palaeolithic Cave Art,* London, Weidenfeld and Nicholson, 1967.

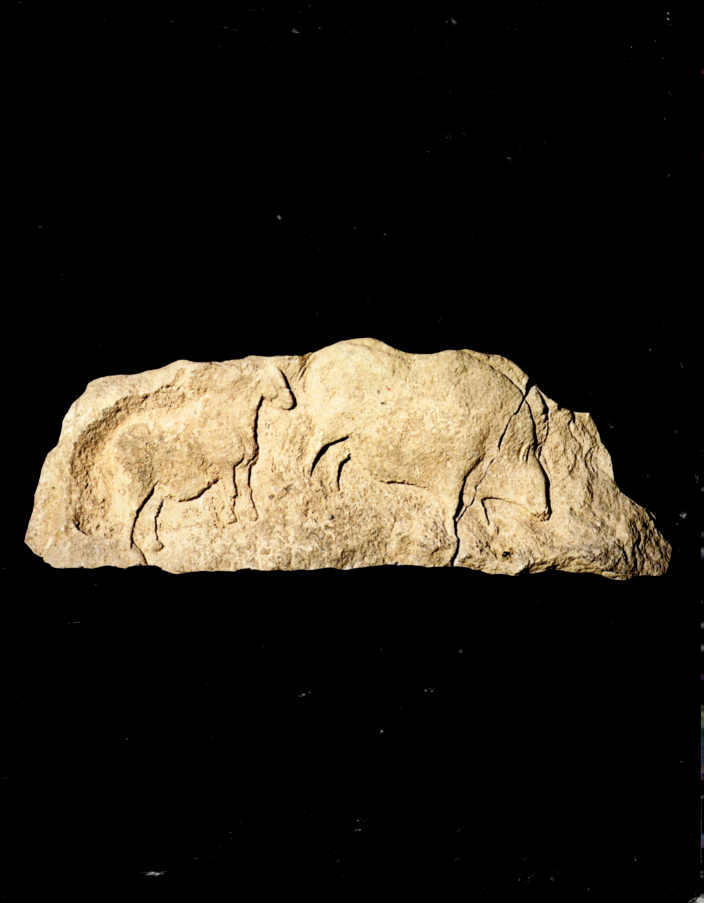

29. *Previous page.* Roc-de-Sers.
Sculpted block.
30. *Top left.* Belcayre. Engraved block.
31. *Lower left.* Ebbou. Ibex engraved
with a simple line.
32. *Right.* Rouffignac. Meanders drawn
with the fingers on a red background.

33. Mountespan. Horse engraved on clay. The modelling
is achieved by the softening of the inner edge of the
engraved line.

34. Commarque.
Large horse's head.
Along the forehead the
engraved line and the
contrast between the
outer and inner edges
can clearly be seen.

35. Tibiran. A series of concretions suggestive of a bear.

36. Montespan. Natural relief transformed into an animal head.

37. Niaux. At the bottom of Assemblage 2 in the Salon Noir, a hollow roughly the shape of a deer's head has been complemented with antlers in black.

38. *Top*. Le Mas-d'Azil.
Head of a bison
scratched on a natural
surface.

39. *Left*. Le Portel.
Human silhouette
centred on a stalactite.

40. *Top left*. Small pieces of iron oxide and manganese. They were scraped on a rough stone to obtain a colouring powder.
41. *Lower left.* Arcy-sur-Cure. Palette charged with ochre.
42. *Right.* Lascaux. The so-called 'Chinese' horse, coloured with blended spots.

43. *Previous page.* Niaux, Salon Noir. Small horse from panel II.

44. *Top left.* Abri Castanet. Details of strongly geometricised female figures. Aurignacian II.

45. *Lower left.* Abri Cellier. The head of an animal associated with a Magdalenian symbol.

46. *Right.* Le Souci. Head of an awl with four small horses in a line, heads to the right. The butt of the object has a fifth horse turning left.

47. Altamira. Geometric sign on the wall of the deep gallery.

48. *Right.* La Baume Latrone. Proboscidean (probably mammoth).
49. *Above.* Isturitz. Horse engraved on a spear point.

50. *Top.* Another version of a proboscidean. The La Baume Latrone figures are archaic in treatment, partly because of technique.
51. *Below.* Las Chimeneas. Deer treated very stylistically.

52. *Top.* Ekaïn. Horse.
53. *Below.* Teyjat. Bull.
54. *Next page.* Lascaux, Nave. The black cow superimposed
on several horses. *(Collection A. Glory)*

55. *Top left.* Mouthiers. Bison recut and transformed into
two horses.
56. *Lower left.* Le Cap Blanc. Low relief of a horse recut as
a bison.
57. *Above.* Lascaux, Room of the Bulls. Horse. (*Collection
A. Glory*)

58. *Top left.* Niaux, Salon Noir, panel IV.
59. *Middle left.* Grotte Chabot.
Mammoth fitted into a field between two
joints of stratification.
60. *Lower left.* Le Portel, small plaque.
Bear fitted into the whole field.
61. *Right.* Limeuil. Reindeer fitted on a
corner.

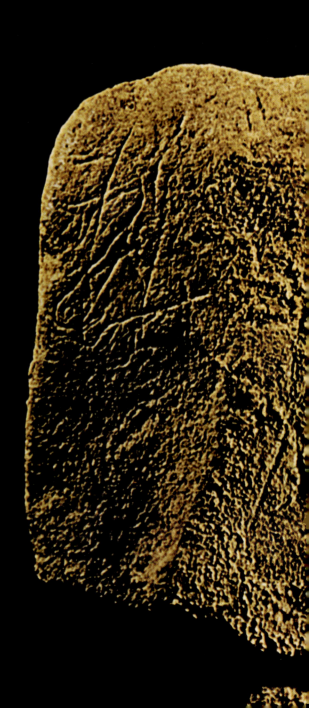

62. *Top*. Rouffignac. Mammoths facing each other.
63. *Below*. La Magdelaine. Elongated women. Left hand
wall and right hand wall.

64. Cougnac. A pair of ibexes.

65. *Top left.* Pech-Merle. Horse, aurochs and bisons without perpendiculars or defined ground surface.
66. *Middle left.* Le Portel, at the forking of galleries 3 and 2. Horse climbing the slope of a small natural ledge.
67. *Lower left.* Rouffignac. A line of mammoths.
68. *Right.* Altxerri. Bison positioned vertically.

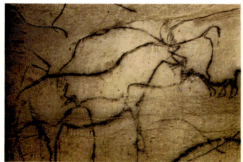

69. Font-de-Gaume. Bison with feet resting on a natural ledge.

70. *Above*. Lascaux, Rotunda. Bull.
71. *Right*. Santimamine. Bison.

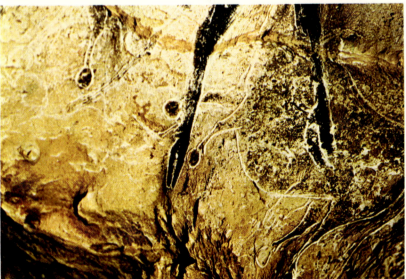

72. *Above.* Lascaux. Horses with oval hooves.
73. *Left.* Lascaux. Forelegs of the black cow, round hooves.

74. *Above left.* Niaux. Wounded bison in style IV.
75. *Above right.* Tassili, Jabbaren. *(Photograph D. Lajoux)*
76. *Lower left.* La Grèze. Bison in style II.
77. *Lower right.* Lascaux. Bichrome stag. *(Collection A. Glory)*
78. *Following page.* Altamira. Bison with an upright tail.

79. *Preceding page.* Lascaux. Chinese horse.
80. *Top left.* Le Portel. Bison. 81. *Middle left.* Pech-Merle. Red horse. 82. *Lower left.* Ebbou. Horse. 83. *Top right.* Le Gabillou. Deer. 84. *Lower right.* Lascaux, Axial Passage. Horse and horns.

85. *Top left.* Lascaux. Bisons crossing.
86. *Middle left.* Le Portel. Bisons crossing?
87. *Lower left.* Lascaux, passage. Horse 110 with bent fetlock.
88. *Right.* Lascaux, passage. Horse 110, detail. *(Photograph D. Vialou)*

89. *Top left.* La Loja. Four aurochs and a horse.
90. *Middle left.* Ekaïn. Horse.
91. *Lower left.* Ebbou. Bison.
92. *Right.* Lascaux. Polychrome horse.
93. *Following page.* Lascaux, shaft. Man overturned by bison. *(Collection A. Glory)*

Two preceding pages: 94. Font-de-Gaume.
Bison.
95. Lascaux, Axial Passage. Red cow.
96. *Top left.* Rouffignac. Mammoth.
97. *Lower left.* Les Combarelles. Reindeer.
98. *Right.* Lascaux. Belling stag. *(Collection
A. Glory)*

99. Marsoulas.
Human face.

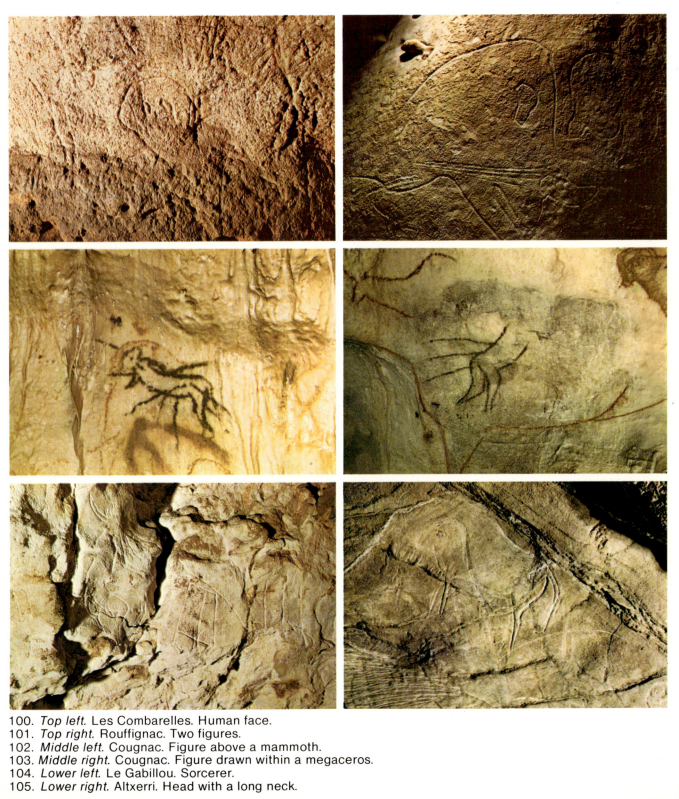

100. *Top left.* Les Combarelles. Human face.
101. *Top right.* Rouffignac. Two figures.
102. *Middle left.* Cougnac. Figure above a mammoth.
103. *Middle right.* Cougnac. Figure drawn within a megaceros.
104. *Lower left.* Le Gabillou. Sorcerer.
105. *Lower right.* Altxerri. Head with a long neck.

106. *Top left.* Pech-Merle. Bird-shaped figure.
107. *Middle left.* La Mouthe. Quadrilateral.
108. *Lower left.* Rouffignac. Roof shape.
109. *Right.* Lascaux. Ibexes facing each other.

110. Pech-Merle. Hand.

111. Gargas.
    Hands.

On the two preceding pages:
Left hand page
112. *Top left.* Niaux. Fissure stained with ochre.
113. *Lower left.* Pech-Merle. Woman-bison.
114. *Top right.* Niaux, Elastres Gallery. Bison.
115. *Middle right.* Cougnac. Deer.
116. *Lower right.* Pech-Merle. Stylised deer.
Right hand page
117. *Top left.* Cougnac. Megaceri.
118. *Middle left.* Santimamine. Bear.
119. *Lower left.* Santimamine. Main panel.
120. *Top right.* Pech-Merle. Black frieze, left side.
121. *Middle right.* Detail of black frieze. Animal drawn in fine outline.
122. *Lower right.* Black frieze. Wounded cow.

This page:
123. *Top left.* Venta de la Perra. Bear.
124. *Top right.* Rouffignac. Rhinoceros.
125. *Lower left.* Lascaux. Wild cat.
126. *Lower right.* Gorge d'Enfer. Fish.

127. *Top left.* Le Portal. Civet.
128. *Top right.* Les Combarelles. Antelope.
129. *Lower left.* Altxerri. Fish.
130. *Lower right.* Altamira. Wild pig.
On the next two pages:
131. Santimamine. Fissure dividing the composition into two. On the left animal figures can be seen.
132. Pech-Merle. Passage of the women-bisons.

DATE DUE

SEP 2 6 1985

SE

DEC 1 2 1985

NOV 5 1986

NOV 1 8 1990

FEB 5 2001

FEB 05 2007

DEMCO 38-297